FAVORITE SERMONS OF

John A. Broadus

FAVORITE SERMONS OF

John A. Broadus

Edited with an Introduction by

VERNON LATRELLE STANFIELD

H|B

HARPER & BROTHERS PUBLISHERS

New York

FAVORITE SERMONS OF JOHN A. BROADUS

FIRST EDITION

D–I

Library of Congress catalog card number: 59–7148

CONTENTS

FOREWORD

DURING his ministry Dr. John A. Broadus published only one brief volume of sermons. Many who have studied his *Treatise on the Preparation and Delivery of Sermons* have wished for more examples of his preaching. Because Dr. Broadus did not write most of his sermons in complete manuscript form, these examples have not been available.

However, Dr. Broadus did leave a box containing sermon materials. An investigation of the contents of this box revealed a number of complete sermon manuscripts and over three hundred sermon briefs and outlines. These sermon briefs will give only a partial picture of the sermons of Broadus, but this incomplete picture will give some indication of how Broadus practiced his theory.

Dr. Broadus' "Day Book" (a record of when and where sermons were preached), shows that these sermons were preached many times. The book might be called "Sermons on Great Texts," for Dr. Broadus took his own counsel and did "not avoid the great texts."

The sermons included in the book may be divided into three classes. There are four sermons from the early book, *Sermons and Addresses;* eight other complete sermons; and twelve sermon briefs. The last two groups are previously unpublished materials.

My debt to others for encouragement and assistance is great. To Dr. J. B. Weatherspoon, my teacher and colleague, who gave me the Broadus material; to William Schoenberg of Harper & Brothers, who gave me encouragement; to the Administrative Services Office of the Southern Baptist Theological Seminary for typing and other assistance—to these and to others, I am deeply grateful.

V. L. STANFIELD

Louisville, Kentucky
January, 1959

FAVORITE SERMONS OF

John A. Broadus

INTRODUCTION

JOHN ALBERT BROADUS: PREACHER EXTRAORDINARY

DURING the last half of the nineteenth century in America, no Baptist preacher enjoyed greater popular fame than did John Albert Broadus. By his Seminary colleagues, by denominational leaders, by competent critics of preaching, and by appreciative congregations, he was ranked as one of the leading preachers of his time.

W. C. Wilkinson, a keen, analytic student of preachers and preaching, gave this appraisal of Dr. Broadus in *Modern Masters of Pulpit Discourse:*

> I have named in my title a man with every natural endowment, every acquired accomplishment, except, perhaps plentitude of physical power, to have become, had he been only a preacher, a preacher hardly second to any in the world.
> . . . His preaching work has been incidental, rather than principal in his career. He presents a conspicuous example . . . of a man who, notwithstanding that this must be said of him, yet enjoys, and justly enjoys . . . a national reputation as a preacher.[1]

In discussing Broadus as a preacher, Dr. A. T. Robertson made this helpful comparison:

> It has been my fortune to hear Beecher and Phillips Brooks, Maclaren, Joseph Parker and Spurgeon, John Hall and Moody, John Clifford and David Lloyd George. At his best and in a congenial atmosphere Broadus was the equal of any man I have ever heard.[2]

In a recent book on the Yale Lectures, *The Royalty of the Pulpit,* Edgar DeWitt Jones has listed Dr. Broadus as one of the Olympians.

[1] William Cleaver Wilkinson, *Modern Masters of Pulpit Discourse* (Philadelphia: The Judson Press, 1905), p. 344.
[2] A. T. Robertson, *The Minister and His Greek New Testament* (New York: George H. Doran Co., 1923), p. 118.

In speaking of the conspicuous position which he occupied and of the esteem and affection in which he was held by Baptists everywhere, Jones observed, "No king on his throne had more loyal and willing subjects than did this professor-preacher." [3]

To these evaluations could be added the personal testimonies of thousands who heard John A. Broadus preach. His fame as a preacher began in his first pastorate at Charlottesville, Virginia, and continued and increased throughout his life. While teaching in the Seminary he was offered some of the leading pastorates in the United States. He was also widely sought as a summer supply—preaching in Richmond, New York, Brooklyn, Detroit, St. Louis, Boston, Philadelphia, Baltimore, and other cities. Dr. Broadus records that he preached seventy-five times as summer supply and on special occasions in Orange, New Jersey. In addition to supply preaching, he delivered many dedication, convention, and commencement sermons, and was the featured speaker at various conferences. Wherever he preached the testimony was the same, "He is one of the world's great preachers."

Since it is most unusual for a preacher to receive almost universal acclaim, a question naturally presents itself. How can one account for the unusual popularity? Actually, this question can never be completely or accurately answered. In every area, but especially in the area of preaching, there is a quality which escapes definition or explanation. However, certain factors in the life of Broadus and in his preaching blended to produce a man with unique preaching abilities.

John Albert Broadus was born January 24, 1827, in Culpepper County, Virginia, the fourth child of Major Edmund Broadus and Nancy Sims. Although the Broadus home was not financially wealthy, it was rich in the things which count—intelligence, culture, love, and piety.

Since John Albert was the youngest child, the parents and the other children shared in his early training. To their instructions was added the teaching of other tutors. From an uncle, Albert G. Sims, he received a careful and accurate grounding in the rudiments of learning. His "graduation" from his uncle's school was somewhat unusual. He returned home unexpectedly and when Major Broadus inquired the reason, his son replied, "My uncle says he has no further use for me." [4] Unable to induce his son to say more, Major Broadus went at

[3] Edgar DeWitt Jones, *The Royalty of the Pulpit* (New York: Harper & Brothers, 1951), p. 51.

[4] A. T. Robertson, *Life and Letters of John Albert Broadus* (Philadelphia: American Baptist Publication Society, 1901), p. 33.

once to see Mr. Sims. However, the boy's uncle assured him that there had been no difficulty, but rather he had taught John "all that he knew."

When he was about sixteen, the young man surrendered himself to Jesus Christ as his Lord and Savior. Though he had been surrounded by religious influences, he had not yet confessed faith in Christ. During a revival meeting at the Mt. Poney Baptist Church, a friend asked him if he would not accept the promise of the preacher's text, "all that the Father giveth me shall come to me. And him that cometh to me I will in no wise cast out." [5] In that moment he yielded his life to Christ. After this initial experience, he made a constant effort to grow in grace and knowledge of his Lord. He began immediately to witness, to study, and to serve. His preaching knew the undergirding of a warm, contagious, experimental religious faith.

From 1844 to 1846 he continued his education by teaching in a small school and engaging in disciplined independent study. It was during this period that he began a study of Greek. It required vast resolution for him to stay by the task. In the development of his religious life, he became a Sunday school teacher and later superintendent. He gave some consideration to becoming a minister, but finally chose medicine and began to make general preparation in that area. Plans were now made for him to enter the University of Virginia.

However, before entering the University his vocational plans were completely changed. He attended an associational meeting and heard a powerful and impressive sermon on the parable of the talents by S. M. Poindexter, one of the most famous preachers in the South. Broadus gave this account of the experience. The preacher

spoke of consecrating one's mental gifts and possible attainments to the work of the ministry. He seemed to clear up all difficulties pertaining to the subject; he swept away all the excuses of fancied humility; he held up the thought that the greatest sacrifices and toils possible to the minister's lifetime would be a hundred-fold repaid if he should be the instrument of saving one soul . . . when the intermission came, the young man . . . sought out his pastor, and with choking voice said: "Brother Grimsley, the question is decided; I must try to be a preacher." [6]

In the fall of 1846, young Broadus entered the University of Virginia as he had planned. His early education had been somewhat irregular; consequently, he spent four years in diligent, disciplined study.

[5] *Loc. cit.*
[6] John A. Broadus, *Sermons and Addresses* (Baltimore: H. M. Wharton and Co., 1886), pp. 398–99.

He received the M.A. degree in 1850 and later came to be considered the University of Virginia's most famous alumnus. At the close of his University course, Broadus declined various offers because he desired to pursue theological studies. During the next year he taught in a private school in Fluvanna County, Virginia, preached in small country churches, and diligently studied church history, theology, sermons, and above all the Bible. During this year two notable events occurred —his ordination August 12, 1850, and his marriage to Miss Maria Harrison, November 13, 1850.

Calls of various kinds came to the young teacher, and he finally accepted the one to be tutor in Latin and Greek at his alma mater and pastor of the Baptist Church at Charlottesville. After one year he resigned his teaching position in order to devote his full time to his pastorate, which he did with the exception of two years when he was given a leave of absence to serve as chaplain at the University of Virginia.

In 1858 he was asked to become a member of the first faculty of the new Southern Baptist Theological Seminary. Though Broadus had had a part in the planning of the institution, he at first declined the offer because of his attachment to preaching and pastoral work. But there ensued months of struggle with himself over the decision, and he finally agreed to become a member of the first faculty of the Seminary when it opened in Greenville, South Carolina, in 1859. For the next thirty-six years, he was Professor of New Testament Interpretation and Homiletics, and his life was inextricably bound to the school.

During the first two years, the Seminary showed real promise, but then came the Civil War and the school was forced to close. Broadus preached in small churches and spent some time as chaplain in Lee's army in Northern Virginia. When the Seminary reopened in 1865, its small endowment was gone, the students few, and the prospect one of struggle and sacrifice. During the darkest days in Greenville, Broadus revealed his spirit when he said to the other professors, "Perhaps the Seminary may die, but let us resolve to die first." However, it was in this period of stress and strain, that Broadus did some of his best and most painstaking work, once carefully reworking his lectures on homiletics for a blind student. In 1870 he published *A Treatise on the Preparation and Delivery of Sermons,* a book which was to become and remain a classic in its field.

The Seminary was moved to Louisville in 1877. Though conditions were somewhat better, Broadus and James P. Boyce, the Seminary's first president, were to give their lives trying to establish the Seminary on a firm financial foundation. Broadus was offered many influential pastorates in the North and South, many professorships and other positions, but he had cast his lot with the school and with it he chose to remain.

The last years of his life were years of increasing fame and recognition. In 1889, he gave the Lyman Beecher Lectures on Preaching at Yale University, the only Southern Baptist ever to be accorded this honor and became the Southern Baptist Theological Seminary's second president. His *Commentary on Matthew, Lectures on the History of Preaching, Harmony of the Gospels,* and other books were to add to his stature as a scholar.

Broadus had struggled with ill health since his college days. By extreme care he had continued his work in spite of toil and trial. However, years of privation and struggle had taken their toll, and Broadus died March 16, 1895, almost at the zenith of his fame. His life had been a life of quiet but intense dedication to a great task.

Now let us turn to the preaching of Broadus. In the preparation of the sermons, the sermons themselves and their delivery, several factors contributed to his unusual pulpit effectiveness.

One factor which contributed to Broadus' power in preaching came from his devotion to God's message. His commission to preach was a commission to speak for God. He had a "profound personal belief in the divine inspiration and authority of the Bible. . . . His reverence for the word of God was one of the deepest feelings of his nature." [7] So eager was he to know the meaning of the Scripture that he began independently the study of Greek and Hebrew. It was not unusual for him in the midst of a sermon to make a plea for the Bible—its worth, its spiritual guidance, its help in attaining holiness. He felt that the Bible was the source of the most potent and precious truth, and in discussing spiritual matters he would say, "We can learn about such a subject as this only from the Bible." [8] One could not do a nobler deed, he believed, than to share the truth of the Bible. In a sermon on the "Holy Scriptures" he said:

> The greatest privilege of earthly life is to give some fellow creature the blessed word of God, and then try by loving speech and example, to bring home to the heart and conscience . . . the truths it contains.[9]

Having this high regard for the Bible, he desired to interpret it

[7] Edwin Charles Dargan, "John Albert Broadus—Scholar and Preacher," *The Crozier Quarterly* (April, 1925), pp. 171–72.
[8] Sermon on I John 1:7.
[9] Broadus, *op. cit.,* pp. 165–66.

rightly. In his textbook, he devoted a brief section to hermeneutics, suggesting ways and means by which the preacher can interpret correctly. One of his favorite injunctions to his class was, "If you forget everything else I have told you, don't forget to treat the Scripture in a common-sense way." [10] Even in a sermon, Dr. Broadus would leave his main idea to make a plea for correct interpretation. In discussing Romans 9:3, "For I could wish that myself were accursed from Christ for my brethren," a text which he said was difficult to interpret, he gave these three rules of interpretation:

> Be willing to let the Scripture mean what it wants to mean . . .
> Take good account of the connection.
> Take good account of the state of the writer's mind.[11]

In his last New Testament class, in which he had lectured on Apollos, he appealed to his students to be "mighty in the Scriptures."

In his own preaching, Dr. Broadus made excellent use of the Scripture. He used a text for every sermon; and the text was more than a springboard; it had a vital relation to the sermon. Sometimes the text would provide the outline of the sermon, sometimes only a portion of the outline, sometimes the subject of the discourse, or again the introduction. He used, never abused, the Scripture.

The texts which he used most frequently are some of the great preaching texts of the Bible. He followed his own advice, "Do not avoid a text because it is familiar." [12] A listing of these texts sounds like a roll call of the great texts of the Bible. This may be seen by noting the texts of the sermons in this book. Surprisingly, however, few of Dr. Broadus' sermons were expository, i.e., drawing the divisions and explanation of the divisions from the text. In fact, he did not often take a long passage as a text. From 1857 to 1893, he kept a record in his "Day Book" of four hundred and sixty sermons which he preached in various places. Of these sermons, 344 were on single verses, 110 on two or more verses, and six were on multiple texts.

Nonetheless, Dr. Broadus was an expository preacher in the broad sense of that term. He rarely, indeed if ever, preached a sermon in which there was not some exposition. He wanted the Scripture to say what it meant; he wanted his listeners to know what God was saying to them. Almost every sermon included here illustrates this concern.

---

[10] J. D. Robertson, "Quotations from the Class Room of Dr. Broadus," in *Seminary Magazine* (April, 1895), p. 428.

[11] Broadus, *op. cit.*, pp. 110–11.

[12] Broadus, *A Treatise on the Preparation and Delivery of Sermons* (Philadelphia: Smith, English and Co., 1872), p. 46.

Because he let himself be a channel of God's message, the intrinsic power of that message gave him unusual power.

A second factor which contributed to his power was the simplicity of his preaching. What he had to say was transparently clear. This does not mean that his sermons lacked worth-while thought. He gave to his preaching his best intellectual effort, but he invariably concealed the processes and brought to his congregations the results of his investigations in language which they could understand. One Sunday morning he preached on the "Practical Aspects of the Trinity," and a ten-year-old boy came forward after the service to thank him for the helpful message.

In the practice of simplicity, Dr. Broadus' practice was in accord with his theory. He called perspicuity "the most important property of style," [13] and felt the preacher had a responsibility to attain it.

A preacher is more solemnly bound than any other person, to make his language perspicuous. This is very important in wording a law, in writing a title-deed, or a physician's prescription, but still more important in proclaiming the word of God, words of eternal life.[14]

This teaching concerning clearness was practice before it became theory. Clarity was a prerequisite in his first pastorate. In the congregation at Charlottesville there were five distinct groups—those from the University, the business people in the town, the country people, the children, and a large group of slaves. Consequently, "he had to give his audience high thinking in simple language." [15] The ideas had to be strong enough to interest the University teachers and clear enough for the others to understand. "He accomplished his feat and made each group, not to say each individual, feel that every sermon was a special message to that class." [16] This lesson once mastered became the rule of his later preaching.

Simplicity can be seen in every aspect of Dr. Broadus' sermon making. His sermon outlines are almost astoundingly simple. The following outline is a sermon on *Repentance* which he recorded having preached nineteen times. It is a simple adverbial plan.

    I. What is it to repent?
    II. Why should we repent?

---

[13] *Ibid.*, p. 339.
[14] *Ibid.*, p. 340.
[15] A. T. Robertson, *op. cit.*, p. 130.
[16] *Loc. cit.*

III.   When shall we repent? [17]

Such simplicity, which is so marked in his organization, is also to
be found in his explanation of terms and ideas. So prominent was the
quality of simplicity that almost any paragraph selected gives evidence of it. A representative example is his explanation of justification:

> What does Paul mean, when he talks about being justified? There has
> been a great deal of misapprehension as to his meaning. Martin Luther
> was all wrong in his early life because he had been reared upon the idea
> that a justified man means simply a just man, a good man, and that he
> could not account himself justified or hope for salvation until he was a
> thorough good man. Now, the Latin word from which we borrow our
> word "justified" does mean *to make just,* and as the Romanists use the
> Latin, their error is natural. But Paul's Greek word means not to *make*
> just, but to *regard* as just, to treat as just. That is a very important differ-
> ence, —not to make just, but to regard and treat as just. How would God
> treat you, if you were a righteous man; if you had, through all your life,
> faithfully performed all your duties, conforming to all your relations to
> your fellow-beings, —how would he regard you and treat you? He would
> look upon you with complacency. He would smile on you as one that was
> in his sight pleasing. He would bless you as long as you lived in this world,
> and, when you were done with this world, he would delight to take you
> home to his bosom, in another world, because you would deserve it. And
> now as God would treat a man who was just because he deserved it, so the
> Gospel proposes to treat men who are not just and who do not deserve it,
> if they believe in the Lord Jesus Christ. He will treat them as just, though
> they are not just, if they believe in Christ; that is to say, he will look upon
> them with his favor; he will smile upon them in his love; he will bless them
> with every good as long as they live, and when they die he will delight to
> take them home to his own bosom, though they never deserved it, through
> his Son, Jesus Christ. That is what Paul means by justification.[18]

So simple were Dr. Broadus' sermons that some people were disappointed the first time they heard him preach. His simple language did
not match his great reputation. However, as they pondered his message, they were eager to hear him a second time.

But here was no artless simplicity; it was the result of studious care.
Dr. Broadus labored to make his message simple. He had learned
from experience that the simple message was acceptable to every
group. (One Sunday he preached a sermon to his congregation at
Cedar Grove, a small country church in South Carolina; a week later
he preached the same sermon at the Southern Baptist Convention in

[17] Unpublished sermon brief on Acts 3:17.
[18] Broadus, *Sermons and Addresses,* pp. 87–88.

Atlanta, Georgia.) He believed strongly in clarity of thought and expression. In an article on "The American Baptist Ministry 100 Years
Ago," he exclaimed, "Alas! for the education of the ministers of Jesus
if it ceases to be true that the common people hear them gladly." [19]
He urged his students to cultivate clarity as a quality of style. Surely,
this purposeful simplicity of style, which made his preaching under-
standable to every audience, was one of the factors which made his
preaching so universally acceptable.

A third factor which contributed to his power was his conscious
purpose to lead his hearers to some spiritual decision. He was not
content just to preach a sermon; he wanted the sermon to do something. In defining good preaching, he declared, "There must be a
powerful impulse upon the will; the hearers must feel smitten, stirred,
moved to, or at least towards, some action or determination to act." [20]
This attitude also is seen in a plea which he frequently made to his
students. "A good speech is a good thing, but the verdict is the thing.
Gentlemen, when you preach strike for a verdict." [21] Dr. W. H. Whitsitt has well summarized the aim which undergirded Broadus' preaching:

In his conception the supreme end of delivery was not to charm or delight the hearer, but rather to convince and persuade him. Therefore,
every art of persuasion was studied and employed if by any means he
might reach the heart and move to action.[22]

Different means were employed to attain this meaningful objective.
Broadus always sought to win the sympathy of his audience. It was
his conviction that the success of a discourse depended largely upon
"the sympathy which one succeeds in gaining from those he addresses." [23] Said he, "if I were asked what is the first thing in effective
preaching, I should say sympathy; and what is the second thing, I
should say sympathy; and what is the third thing, sympathy.[24]

Perhaps the most effective means he used to win immediate ver-
dicts, however, was direct appeal. Dr. Broadus knew how to make
direct appeal—not in a bombastic, overbearing way, but in a quiet,

[19] *Baptist Quarterly* (January, 1875), p. 17.
[20] *A Treatise on the Preparation and Delivery of Sermons,* p. 20.
[21] J. D. Robertson, *op. cit.,* p. 430.
[22] W. H. Whitsitt, "John Albert Broadus," *Review and Expositor* (July,
1907), p. 347.
[23] *Sermons and Addresses,* p. 37.
[24] *Loc. cit.*

winning way. Sometimes this appeal came within the body of the sermon, but generally it came as part of a conclusion.

Examples of his use of direct appeal as a method of conclusion are numerous. A representative example is seen in a part of the conclusion in a sermon, "Ask and It Shall Be Given You." After a long conclusion, he makes a final appeal:

> My friends, let us make it a practical lesson for us all. Christian people, begin to pray more. Fathers of families, if you have neglected to pray with your families, begin now at once. If you have been negligent in public or private prayer, renew your petitions with earnestness. O, troubled one, shrinking away from the Saviour, remember that he said, "Ask and it shall be given you." And, if there is somebody here this evening that has not prayed for months, that has not prayed for years; if there is some man that has not prayed since the time long ago when he prayed by his mother's knee, and who all these years has been slighting God's word and rejecting God's invitation; O soul, O fellow-sinner, will you not to-night take Jesus' word home to your heart, and begin to find in your experience what some like you have found, that you have but to ask and it shall be given.[25]

The use of direct appeal is sometimes resented by an audience —but not when used in the spirit in which Broadus used it. His audiences felt a great soul yearning for their spiritual good. His appeals were motivated by love, and as genuine love always does, that love drew a response.

These are the means which Dr. Broadus used to lead his listeners to make spiritual decisions. In a lesser man they could have been only techniques, ends in themselves; but as used by Broadus, they were means to achieve a high end—that of helping his hearers.

A fourth factor which contributed to Broadus' preaching power was his method of preparation and delivery. Early in his ministry, Dr. Broadus determined to master the technique of preaching. Besides his own dedication to his task, the high standard for sermon delivery which had been established in Virginia, the demands of a university church, and perhaps the example set by Andrew Broadus, his famous kinsman, spurred him to attain his best. Consequently, long before he had thought of teaching homiletics, he began an analytic study of the great preachers and their sermons and sought to put the principles which he learned from them into practice. In 1854 Dr. Broadus wrote an article for the *Religious Herald* on the "Best Mode of Preparing and Delivering Sermons." This article, which was a forerunner of his later book, set forth his ideals of sermon preparation and delivery.

Dr. Broadus had unique methods of making preparation for the

[25] *Ibid.*, pp. 68–69.

pulpit. As a result of his severe discipline in independent study, he had, even as a young man, a large fund of general knowledge to draw upon. He not only sought to master his favorite studies, the Bible and ancient and modern languages, but he read widely in history, philosophy, art, literature, and current events. These studies strengthened and elevated the powers of mind and modes of expression and gave him a large mental store upon which to draw in sermon preparation. In his immediate preparation, he would take a text, seek to find its exact meaning, and then arrange its ideas under logical headings. Since Dr. Broadus "preferred speaking to writing as a mode of self-expression," [26] he wrote little. He would jot down introductory ideas, state his main points clearly, and indicate his illustrations. Such brief writing was usually done on a sheet of writing paper, folded lengthwise, making four long, narrow pages. When typed, one of these sermons makes a manuscript three to six pages in length. A typical sheet showing his handwriting is reproduced on p. 141.

His method of preparation has often been criticized, the critics feeling that the sermons should have been fully written. However, Dr. Broadus wanted the freedom of choosing exact words in the act of delivery as the occasion and nature of the subject dictated. Thus he was left free for many striking asides and helpful thoughts which came to him as he spoke. This method proved quite advantageous to Dr. Broadus after he became a seminary professor. Before re-preaching a sermon, he would spend at least two hours trying to adapt it to the new situation and in seeking to make the sermon real to him again.[27] Thus he re-created his sermons and gave them a freshness and vitality which they might not otherwise have had.

After this writing, Dr. Broadus would fix the sermon in his mind by thinking about it as he walked, a habit which he formed early in life. His daughter, Miss Eliza Broadus, recorded that near the University of Virginia he had worn a path by walking back and forth as he prepared to speak.[28] And now he was ready for the sermon prepared to become the sermon delivered. In the essay written in 1854, he maintained that a "sermon becomes such only in the act of delivery. Whatever mode of preparing be adopted, it is not strictly a sermon, but only preparation until it is delivered." [29]

Dr. Broadus did not use the brief notes which he had prepared. He

[26] Dargan, *op. cit.,* p. 171.

[27] A. T. Robertson, *op. cit.,* p. 121.

[28] Eliza Sumerville Broadus, "Some Recollections of My Father," *Western Recorder* (July 25, 1929), p. 4.

[29] John A. Broadus, "On the Best Mode of Preparing and Delivering Sermons," in *Religious Herald* (Dec. 14, 1854), p. 193.

practiced what he called extempore delivery; in fact, he would not carry a "scrap of paper" into the pulpit with him. One Sunday morning as he was walking into the church, he discovered that he had his notes with him. He turned to his daughter, Mrs. A. T. Robertson, and said, "Daughter, I forgot to leave my notes at home. Will you keep them until after the services?" However, extempore delivery did not mean extempore thinking. It meant a free delivery after careful preparation.

Freedom from a manuscript allowed him the freedom to look directly at his audience and establish excellent eye contact. He assiduously cultivated this habit and developed the ability to make each person in the audience feel that he was talking directly to him. Dr. T. M. Hawes, who taught classes in public speaking at the Seminary, said of Dr. Broadus:

> No matter how far away from him you might be, he always seemed near. Somehow he always seemed to be speaking to me, and the others were there simply to hear what he had to say, so great was his power of individualizing an audience.[30]

Contributing also to his directness was his conversational manner of speaking. Broadus always began quietly and easily and continued in a conversational tone. He often urged his students to "talk like folks talk," and he tried to put that rule into practice. In keeping with his quiet delivery, he used few gestures, but these were always appropriate for enforcing his ideas. His voice, while not unusually strong, had wonderful carrying power. It was marked by a soft richness, fine flexibility, and often expressed deep pathos. He articulated carefully and there was a good distribution of emphasis. Though his sermons have been called "enlarged conversations," he would occasionally burst forth spontaneously into intense and blazing declamation. He was capable of eloquence which carried his hearers to heights of thought and emotion.

His quiet conversational delivery brought both critics and imitators. Some men, who equated "real preaching" with soaring in the oratorical stratosphere, accused Broadus of "ruining the preachers of the South" by his example. His students, however, saw his effectiveness, and in spite of his warning, many of them tried to imitate his tones, his genuine pathos, his platform manner, failing to realize that they had only a few of his external characteristics and not the qualities of his success.

[30] T. M. Hawes, "Memories of John A. Broadus," in *Seminary Magazine* (March, 1903), p. 225.

This method of delivery was deeply appreciated by the congregations which heard Broadus speak—for audiences have always appreciated preachers who look directly at them and speak directly to them. His Lyman Beecher Lectures on Preaching, which were delivered in this manner, were enthusiastically received by the students and faculty at Yale University.[31] Since his unique method of preparing and delivering sermons won the same enthusiastic response from every group he addressed, it must be listed as an important element of strength in his preaching. It was, however, the total impact of man and message that made John A. Broadus such a tremendously popular preacher to his own generation. In Broadus, his audience sensed reality. One listener summarized and made articulate what many felt about Broadus' preaching.

It was not so much what he said. It did seem that almost anyone might have said what he was saying. But it was the man behind the message. He spoke with the authority of one who tested and knew the truth.[32]

[31] A. T. Robertson, *Life and Letters of John Albert Broadus*, pp. 376–77.
[32] Claude W. Duke, "Memorial Address of Dr. John A. Broadus," in *Review and Expositor* (April, 1927), p. 172.

1

SOME LAWS OF SPIRITUAL WORK

But he said unto them, I have meat to eat that ye know not.
The disciples therefore said one to another, Hath any man
brought him aught to eat? Jesus saith unto them, My meat is to
do the will of him that sent me, and to accomplish his work. Say
not ye, There are yet four months, and then cometh the harvest?
Behold, I say unto you, Lift up your eyes and look on the fields,
that they are white already unto harvest. He that reapeth receiveth wages, and gathereth fruit unto life eternal; that he that
soweth and he that reapeth may rejoice together. For herein is
the saying true, One soweth, and another reapeth. I sent you to
reap that whereon ye have not labored: others have labored, and
ye are entered into their labor. JOHN 4:32–38

THE disciples must have been very much astonished at the change
which they observed in the Master's appearance. They left him, when
they went away to a neighboring city to buy food, reclining beside
Jacob's well, quite worn out with the fatigue of their journey, following upon the fatigues of long spiritual labors. And here now he is
sitting up, his face animated, his eyes kindled. He has been at work
again. Presently they ask him to partake of the food which they had
brought, and his answer surprised them: "I have food to eat that ye
know not." They looked around, and saw nobody; the woman to
whom he had been speaking was gone, and they said, "Has any one
brought him something to eat?" Jesus answered, "My food is to do
the will of him that sent me, and to accomplish his work." And then,
with this thought of work, he changes the image to sowing and reaping, and bids them go forth to work.

Now, from this passage with its images, I have wished to discourse
upon *some laws of spiritual work,* as here set forth. For we are beginning to see, in our time, that there are laws in the spiritual sphere as
truly as in the mental and in the physical spheres. What are the laws
of spiritual work which the Saviour here indicates? I name four:

I. Spiritual work is *refreshing* to soul and body. "My food is," said

14

the tired, hungry one, who had aroused himself, "to do the will of him that sent me, and to accomplish his work."

We all know the power of the body over the mind, and we all know, I trust, the power of the mind over the body; how any animating theme can kindle the mind until the wearied body will be stirred to new activities; until the man will forget that he was tired, because of that in which he is interested. But it must be something that does deeply interest the mind. So there is suggested to us the thought that we should learn to love spiritual work. If we love spiritual work it will kindle our souls; it will even give health and vigor to our bodies. There are some well-meaning, but good-for-nothing, professed Christians in our time, who would have better health of mind and even better health of body, if they would do more religious work and be good for something in their day and generation.

How shall we learn to love religious work so that it may kindle and refresh us? Old Daniel Sharp, who was a famous Baptist minister in Boston years ago, used to be very fond of repeating, "The only way to learn to preach is to preach." Certainly, the only way to learn to do anything is to *do* the thing. The only way to learn to love spiritual work is to keep doing it until we gain pleasure from the doing; until we discern rewards in connection with the doing; and to cherish all the sentiments which will awaken in us that "enthusiasm of humanity" which it was Jesus that introduced among men; and to love the souls of our fellow men, to love the wandering, misguided lives, to love the suffering and sinning all around us with such an impassioned love that it shall be a delight to us to do them good and to try to save them from death. Then that will refresh both mind and body.

II. There are *seasons* in the spiritual sphere—sowing seasons and reaping seasons, just as there are in farming. "Say not ye," said Jesus, "There are yet four months, and then cometh the harvest?"—that is to say, it was four months from that time till the harvest. They sowed their wheat in December; they began to reap it in April. "Say not ye, There are yet four months, and then cometh the harvest? Behold, I say unto you, Lift up your eyes and look on the fields; for they are white already to harvest."

In the spiritual sphere it was a harvest time then, and they were bidden to go forth and reap the harvest that waved white and perishing. We can see, as we look back, that the ends of all the ages had now come to that time; that the long course of providential preparation, dimly outlined in the Old Testament, had led to the state of things that then prevailed; that the fullness of the times had come, when God sent forth his Son to teach men and to atone for men, and to rise again and come forth as their Saviour, and that his servants should go forth in his name. And the like has been true in many other seasons of Christianity; there have been great reaping times, when men have harvested the fruits which come from the seed scattered by others long before.

This principle is true in individual churches, that there are seasons of sowing and reaping. It has to be so. We sometimes say we do not believe in the revival idea; we think there ought to be revival in the church all the time. If you mean that we ought always to be seeking for spiritual fruits, always aiming at spiritual advancement, it is true. But if you mean that you expect that piety will go on with even current in the church, that there will be just as much sowing and reaping at any one time as at any other, then you will certainly be disappointed. That is not the law of human nature. That is not possible in the world. Periodicity pervades the universe. Periodicity controls the life of all individuals, shows itself in the operations of our minds. Periodicity necessarily appears in the spiritual sphere also. People have their ups and downs. They ought to strive against falling low. They ought not to be content with growing cold. They ought to seek to maintain good health of body all the while, but it will not be always equally good; and good health of mind and soul all the time, but it will not be always equally good. They ought to be seeking to reap a harvest of spiritual good among those around them all the while; but they will have seasons which are rather of sowing, and other seasons which will be rather of reaping.

Oh! do you want to see a great season of harvest among your own congregation? And do you not know, brethren, as well as the preacher can tell you, what is necessary in order that you may see it? What are the conditions but deepened spiritual life in your own individual souls, stronger spiritual examples set forth in your lives, more earnest spirituality in your homes, a truer standard in your business and social relations to mankind, more of heartfelt prayer of God's blessing, and more untiring and patient and persevering effort, in season and out of season, to bring others to seek their salvation?

III. Spiritual work *links the workers in unity*. "Herein is the saying true," said Jesus; "One soweth, and another reapeth. Other men have labored, and ye are entered into their labors."

The prophets centuries before had been preparing for that day, and the forerunner had been preparing for that day, and the labors of Jesus himself in his early ministry had been preparing the way, and now the disciples could look around them upon fields where, from the sowing of others, there were opportunities for them to reap. "Other men have labored, and ye are entered into their labors. One soweth, and another reapeth." That is the law everywhere; it is true of all the higher work of humanity—"One soweth, and another reapeth"; and our labors link us into unity. It is true of human knowledge. How little has any one individual of mankind been able to find out beyond what the world has known before! Even the great minds that stand like mountain peaks as we look back over the history of human thought, when we come to look into it, do really but uplift the thought that is all around them; else they themselves could not have risen.

It is true in practical inventions. We pride ourselves on the fact that ours is an age of such wonderful practical inventions; we sometimes persuade ourselves that we must be the most intelligent generation of mankind that ever lived, past all comparison; that no other race, no other century, has such wonderful things to boast of. How much of it do we owe to the men of the past! Every practical invention of today has been rendered possible by what seemed to us the feeble attainments of other centuries, by the patient investigation of the men who, in many cases, have passed away and been forgotten. We stand upon the shoulders of the past, and rejoice in our possessions, and boast; and when we grow conceited and proud of it, we arc like a little boy lifted by his father's supporting arms, and standing on his father's shoulders, and clapping his hands above his father's head, and saying, in childish glee, "I am taller than papa!" A childish conclusion, to be sure.

We stand upon the shoulders of the past, and thereby we are lifted up in all the higher work of mankind; and we ought to be grateful to the past, and mindful of our duty to the future; for the time will come when men will look back upon our inventions, our slow travel, our wonderful ignorance of the power of physical forces and the adaptations of them to physical advancement, and smile at the childishness with which, in the fag end of the nineteenth century, we boasted of ourselves and our time.

And now it is not strange that this same thing should be true of spiritual work. When you undertake to do some good in a great city like this, you might sit down and say, "What can I do with all this mass of vice and sin?" But you do not have to work alone. You can associate yourself with other workers, in a church, with various organizations of workers, and thereby re-enforce your own exertions; you can feel that you are a part of a mighty force of workers, of your own name and other Christian names. Grace be with all them that love our Lord Jesus Christ in sincerity, and are trying to do good in his name! And it will cheer our hearts to remember that wide over the land and over the world are unnumbered millions of workers of the army to which we belong. They tell us that the International Sunday School Lessons which most of us study every Sunday are actually studied now every Lord's day by at least ten millions of people, all studying on the same day the same portion of the Bible. That is but one fact to remind us that we are members of a great spiritual host, doing a great work in the world.

And not merely are there many contemporaries with whom we are linked in unity, but we are in unity with the past; other men have labored and we have entered into their labors. All the good that all the devout women and all the zealous men of past ages have been doing has come down to us, opening the way for us to do good. And not merely with the past, but we are linked with the laborers of the future. They may hear our names or they may hear them not. We may perish from all memory of mankind, but our work will not ever, and if we are engaged in the Lord's work, we link ourselves to his permanency and his almightiness, and our work will go down to help the men who are to come after.

The same thing is true here, also, in the individual church; one soweth and another reapeth. A pastor seldom gathers half as much fruit from the seed of his own sowing as he gathers from the seed that others have sown. And there will come some man here—God grant it may be soon, and wisely, and well—who will gather seed from the sowing of the venerable pastor so well and worthily beloved in years ago, seed from the sowing of the energetic pastor of recent years, and O my soul, he may gather some harvest, even from the seed scattered in the brief fleeting interim of this summer. We put all our work together. We sink our work in the one great common work. We scatter seed for God and for souls, and we leave it to God's own care and blessing. One soweth, and another reapeth.

My brethren, there is nothing like Christianity to individualize mankind. It was Christianity that taught us to appreciate the individuality of men: "Every man must give account of himself unto God." Men were no longer to lose themselves in the state, as classical antiquity taught them to do, but to stand out in their separate personality and individual responsibility and individual rights and duties. But at the same time much of what we can do that is best in the world we must do by close connection and interaction one with another. Let us rejoice to act through others.

Priscilla and Aquila! What a power they were for early Christianity when they took that eloquent young Alexandrian Apollos and taught him in private the way of God more perfectly! Priscilla, that devout woman, stood, in fact, before delighted assemblies in Corinth and spoke to them the perfect way of God through the eloquent man whom she had taught. And how often does the Sunday school teacher, who labored long and, as the world might have thought, fruitlessly, with her little naughty boys and girls, become in future times a great power for good in the world through one or other of them! The teacher has to sink himself in his pupils: never mind if he sinks all out of the world's sight, provided he can make his mark upon *them* and prepare them for greater usefulness, and put into them some good spirit, and send them forth to do the work which to him personally is denied.

Here lies the great power of Christian women. There is much they can do personally, with their own voice and their own action, but there is more they can do by that wondrous influence which men vainly strive to depict, that influence over son and brother and husband and friend whereby all the strength and power of the man is softened and guided and sobered and made wiser through the blessed influence of the woman.

God be thanked that we can not only do good in our individual efforts, but we can do good through others! Let us cultivate this, let us delight in this, that we can labor through others. Whenever your pastor may stand before the gathered assembly he can speak with more power because of you, if you do your duty to him and through him.

IV. Spiritual work *has rich rewards.* "And he that reapeth receiveth wages," saith Jesus, "and gathereth fruit unto life eternal."

Spiritual work has rich rewards. It has the reward of success. It is not in vain to try to do good to the souls of men through the truth of God and seeking his grace. Sometimes you may feel as if you were standing at the foot of a precipice a thousand feet high and trying to spring to its summit, and were all powerless. Sometimes you may feel as if you had flung your words against a stone wall and made no impression at all. Sometimes you may go away all ashamed of what you have said in public or in private. But there was never a word spoken that uttered God's truth and sought God's blessing, that was spoken in vain. Somehow it does good to somebody, it does good at some time or other; it shall be known in earth or in heaven that it did do good. Comfort your hearts with these words: It is not in vain to try to do good.

You may say, "I have not the lips of the eloquent, the tongue of the learned, how can I talk?" There is many a minister who is eloquent and has preached to gathered congregations, who could tell you that he knows of many more instances in which his private words have been blest to individuals than he knows of such instances in public. I knew of a girl who had been so afflicted that she could not leave her couch for years, who had to be lifted constantly—poor, helpless creature!—but who would talk to those who came into her room about her joy in God, and would persuade them to seek the consolations of the Gospel, and many were benefited and would bring their friends to her, till after a while they brought them from adjoining counties, that she, the poor, helpless girl, might influence them; at length she even began to write letters to people far away, and that girl's sickbed became a center of blessing to people throughout a whole region.

We talk about doing nothing in the world. Ah, if our hearts were in it! we do not know what we can do. That tiger in the cage has been there since he was a baby tiger, and does not know that he could burst those bars if he were but to exert his strength. Oh, the untried strength in all our churches, and the good that the people could do if we would only try, and keep trying, and pray for God's blessing. My friends, you cannot save your soul as a solitary, and you ought not to dare to try to go alone into the paradise of God. We shall best promote our own piety when we are trying to save others. We shall be most helpful to ourselves when we are most helpful to those around us. Many of you have found it so; and all of you may find it so, again and again, with repetitions that shall pass all human telling. "For he that watereth shall be watered also again."

Spiritual work shall also be rewarded in the Lord of the harvest's commendation and welcome. Ah, he will know which was the sowing and which was the reaping. The world may not know; we may never hear; but he will know which was the sowing and which was the reaping, and who tried to do good and thought he had not done it, and who was sad and bowed down with the thought of being utterly unable to be useful, and yet was useful. He will know, he will reward even the desire of the heart, which there was no opportunity to carry out. He will reward the emotion that trembled on the lip and could find no utterance. He will reward David for wanting to build the temple as well as Solomon for building it. He will reward all that we do, and all that we try to do, and all that we wish to do. O blessed God! he will be your reward and mine, forever and forever.

2

THE HABIT OF THANKFULNESS

In everything give thanks. I Thessalonians 5:18

We hear a great deal said about habits. But it nearly always means bad habits. Why should we not think and speak much about good habits? They are as real, and almost as great, a power for good as bad habits are for evil. We do our work largely by the aid of habit. How much this helps one in playing on an instrument, or writing on a typewriter. Through many a familiar conjunction of notes or of letters the fingers fly with the very smallest amount of attention and exertion. Many a man who is growing old will every day get through an amount of work that surprises his friends, and it is possible because he works in the lines of lifelong habit. Besides, the only possible way to keep out bad habits is to form good habits. By a necessity of our nature, whatever is frequently and at all regularly done becomes habitual. If a man has been the slave of evil habits, and wishes to be permanently free, he must proceed by systematic and persevering effort to establish corresponding good habits. The education of our children, both at school and at home, the self-education of our own early life, consists mainly in the formation of intellectual and moral habits. I think we ought to talk more upon this subject, in public and in private —upon the power and blessing of good habits. And the theme of this discourse will be, the habit of thankfulness to God.

I. Consider the value of the habit of thankfulness.

It tends to quell repining. We are all prone, especially in certain moods, to complain of our lot. Every one of us has at some time or other imagined, and perhaps declared, that he has a particularly hard time in this world. It is to be hoped that in other moods we are heartily ashamed of ourselves for such repining. But how to prevent its recurrence? A most valuable help will be the habit of thankfulness to God. Then if a fretful, repining spirit begins to arise, just in the middle, perhaps, of some complaining sentence, we shall suddenly change to an expression of thankfulness—and perhaps end with laughing at ourselves for the folly of such repining.

It tends to enhance enjoyment. We all know that when we receive a gift, with any true sentiment and any suitable expression of thankfulness, the reaction of gratitude augments our gratification.

It serves to soothe distress. Persons who are greatly afflicted, and not wont to be thankful, sometimes find the memory of past joys only an aggravation of present sorrow. Far otherwise with one who has learned to be habitually thankful. For him the recollection of happier hours is still a comfort.

It helps to allay anxiety. Did you ever notice what the apostle says to the Philippians? "In nothing be anxious; but in everything by prayer and supplication with thanksgiving let your requests be made known unto God. And the peace of God, which passeth all understanding, shall guard your hearts and your thoughts in Christ Jesus." Notice carefully that we are to prevent anxiety by prayer as to the future with thanksgiving for the past.

It cannot fail to deepen penitence. "The goodness of God leadeth thee to repentance." When we are fully in the habit of thankfully observing and recalling the loving-kindnesses and tender mercies of our heavenly Father, this will make us perceive more clearly, and lament more earnestly, the evil of sin against him; and what is more, this will strengthen us to turn from our sins to his blessed service.

It has as one necessary effect to brighten hope. "I love to think on mercies past, And future good implore" is a very natural conjunction of ideas. If we have been wont to set up Ebenezers upon our path of life, then every glance backward along these milestones of God's mercy will help us to look forward with more of humble hope.

It serves to strengthen for endurance and exertion. We all know how much more easily and effectively they work who work cheerfully; and the very nutriment of cheerfulness is found in thankfulness as to the past and hope as to the future.

If this habit of thankfulness to God is so valuable, it is certainly worth our while to consider,

II. Occasions of habitual thankfulness. It is obvious that these are numerous and various beyond description. But we may find profit in summing them all up under two heads.

1. We should be thankful to God for everything that is pleasant. No one will dispute that proposition in theory, whatever may be our practice. The apostle James tells us that "every good gift and every perfect boon is from above, coming down from the Father of lights." We have so much occasion to speak about the religious benefits of affliction, to dwell on the blessed consolations of Christian piety amid the sorrows of life, that we are in danger of overlooking the other

side. It is a religious duty to enjoy to the utmost every rightful pleasure of earthly existence. He who gave us these bodies, so "fearfully and wonderfully made," who created us in his own image, with spirits of such keen appetency and longing aspiration, desires that we should find life a pleasure. As already intimated, we work best at what we enjoy. It is highly important that the young should enjoy what they are studying; and while this may, to some extent, be accomplished by giving them studies they fancy, it is also possible that by well-guided efforts they should learn to relish studies to which they were at first disinclined. I sometimes hear young married people say, "We are going to housekeeping, and then we can have what we like." I sometimes feel at liberty to reply, "Yes, to a certain extent you may; but what is far more important and interesting, you will be apt to like what you have." To have what we like is for the most part an impossible dream of human life; to like what we have is a possibility, and not only a duty, but a high privilege.

2. We should be thankful to God for everything that is painful. Well, that may seem to be stating the matter too strongly. We can help ourselves by noticing that whatever may be possible in that direction, the apostle has not in the text enjoined quite so much as the phrase just used would propose. He does not say, "for everything give thanks," though that might be enjoined; he says, "in everything give thanks." Now that, surely, need not seem impossible.

We may always be thankful that the situation is no worse. The old Negro's philosophy was wise and good: "Bress de Lord, 'taint no wuss." We always deserve that it should be worse, no matter how sorrowful may be the actual situation. We can never allow ourselves to question that with some persons it has been worse. Let us always bless the Lord, that but for his special mercies it would be worse with us today.

I recall an unpublished anecdote of President Madison, told to me in the region where he lived and died. It may be mentioned, by the way, that Mr. Madison was a rarely excellent and blameless man. His biographer told me that, notwithstanding all the political conflicts of a life so long and so distinguished, he found no indication that Mr. Madison's private character had ever been in the slightest degree assailed—an example which it would perhaps be difficult to parallel. In his old age the venerable ex-President suffered from many diseases, took a variety of medicines and contrived to live notwithstanding. An old friend from the adjoining county of Albemarle sent him a box of vegetable pills of his own production, and begged to be informed whether they did not help him. In due time came back one of those carefully written and often felicitous notes for which Mr. Madison and Mr. Jefferson were both famous, to somewhat the following effect: "My dear friend. I thank you very much for the box of pills. I have taken them all; and while I cannot say that I am better since taking them, it is quite possible that I might have been worse if I had not taken them, and so I beg you to accept my sincere acknowledgments." Really, my friends, this is not a mere pleasantry. There is always something, known or unknown, but for which our condition might have been worse, and at the very least, that something constitutes an occasion for gratitude. Whatever we may have lost, there is always something left.

As already observed, our present sufferings may well set in brighter relief the remembered happiness of other days. And though men are prone to make this an occasion of repining, yet it ought to be an occasion of thankfulness. Not long ago a young husband spoke to me, with bitter sorrow, about the death of his wife. I suggested that he might well be thankful for having lived several happy years in the most intimate companionship with one so lovely; and that in coming years, when the blessed alchemy of memory should make her character seem all-perfect in his eyes, he might well find pathetic and ineffable pleasure in the memory of that early time. We all know how to repeat, amid sorrowful recollections, those words of Tennyson, "Oh, death in life, the days that are no more!" But it is surely possible so to cherish blessed and inspiring memories as to invert the line, and say, "Oh, life in death, the days that are no more!"

There is a still more important view of this matter. It has become a blessed commonplace of Christian philosophy that our sufferings may, through the grace of God, be the means of improving our character. Such a result is by no means a matter of course. Sufferings may be so borne, with such bitter repining and selfish brooding, as greatly to damage character. But the Scriptures assure us that devout souls may regard affliction as but a loving Father's chastisement, meant for their highest good. In all the ages there has never been a pious life that did not share this experience. To be exempt from it would, as the Bible expressly declares, give clear proof that we are not children of God at all. Many of us could testify today, if it were appropriate, that the sorrows of life have by God's blessing done us good. All of us have occasion to lay more thoroughly to heart the lessons of affliction. And oh! if we do ever climb the shining hills of glory, and look back with clearer vision upon the strangely mingled joys and sorrows of this earthly life, then how deeply grateful we shall be for those very afflictions, which at the time we find it so hard to endure. If we believe this to be true, and it is a belief clearly founded on

Scripture, then can we not contrive, even amid the severest sufferings, to be thankful for the lessons of sorrow, for the benefits of affliction?

Remember, too, how our seasons of affliction make real to us the blessed thought of divine compassion and sympathy. When you look with parental anguish upon your own suffering child, then you know, as never before, the meaning of those words, "Like as a father pitieth his children, so the Lord pitieth them that fear him." When you find the trials of life hard to bear, then it becomes unspeakably sweet to remember that our High Priest can be touched with the feeling of our infirmities, having been "in all points tempted like as we are, yet without sin." Thus affliction brings to the devout mind blessed views of the divine character, which otherwise we should never fully gain.

> Then sorrow, touched by thee, grows bright
>   With more than rapture's ray;
> As darkness shows us worlds of light
>   We never saw by day.

Besides all this, remember that the sufferings of this present life will but enhance, by their contrast, the blessed exemptions of the life to come. A thousand times have I remembered the text of my first funeral sermon, "And there shall be no more death, neither sorrow nor crying; neither shall there be any more pain: for the former things are passed away." These are the present things now—all around us and within us; but the time is coming when they will be the former things, quite passed away. You know the use which skillful composers make of discords in music. The free use of them is among the characteristics of Wagner; but they are often found in our simplest tunes for public worship. The jarring discord is solved, and makes more sweet the harmony into which it passes. And oh! the time is coming when all the pains and pangs of this present life will seem to have been only "a brief discordant prelude to an everlasting harmony."

My friends, are you optimists or pessimists? Let me explain to the children what those words mean. The Latin word *optimus* means "best," and *pessimus* means "worst." So an Optimist is one who maintains that this is the best possible world; and a Pessimist, that it is the worst possible world. Now which are you, an optimist or a pessimist? For my part, I am neither. Surely no man can really imagine that this is the best possible world, save in some brief moment of dreamy forgetfulness. And as to thinking it the worst possible world—well, a person would have to be uncommonly well off who could afford to think that.

I read, some time ago, a biography of Arthur Schopenhauer, the

celebrated German pessimist. I was not surprised to find that his
father left him an independent fortune, and he had no painful bodily
diseases. He could afford to spend his time in trying to persuade
everybody to be miserable, in building pessimistic theories. But most
of us have so many real toils and troubles that we are instinctively
driven to search for the bright side of life, to seek all possible consolation and cheer. Louis Agassiz had "no time to make money"; and
few of us will ever have time to be pessimists. No, we cannot begin
to say with Pope, "Whatever is, is right"; nor yet to reverse it, "Whatever is, is wrong." But whether poetical or not, it will be a very true
and valuable saying if we read, "Whatever is, you must make the best
of it." And just in proportion as we strive to make the best of everything, we shall find it practicable to carry out the apostle's injunction,
"In everything give thanks."

The greatest of early Christian preachers, perhaps the greatest in
all Christian history, was Chrysostom. His motto was, "Glory to God
for all things." He probably derived it from the story of Job, which
was his favorite subject of devout meditation, and is mentioned in a
large proportion of his eloquent sermons. You might fancy that it
was easy for the young man to say, "Glory to God for all things,"
when he was growing up in Antioch, the idol of his widowed mother,
with ample means, and the finest instructors of the age. You might
think it easy to say this when he was a famous preacher, in Antioch,
and afterwards in Constantinople, when ten thousand people crowded
the great churches to hear him; though such a preacher could not
fail to suffer profoundly through compassion for the perishing, and
anxious effort to reclaim the wandering, and sympathy for all the
distressed, as well as with many a pang of grief and shame that he did
not preach better. But Chrysostom continued to say this, when the
Court at Constantinople turned against him, when the wicked
Empress became his enemy, and compassed his banishment again
and again. When his friends would go to far Armenia and visit him in
exile, he would say to them, "Glory to God for all things." When he
was sent to more distant and inhospitable regions, so as to be out of
reach of such pious visiting, his letters were apt to end, "Glory to
God for all things." And when the soldiers were dragging him through
winter snows, and, utterly worn out, he begged to be taken into a
little wayside church that he might die, his last words, as he lay on
the cold stone floor, were, "Glory to God for all things."

III. How may the habit of thankfulness be formed and maintained?
Well, how do we form other habits? If you wish to establish the habit
of doing a certain thing, you take pains to do that thing, upon every

possible occasion, and to avoid everything inconsistent therewith. Now, then, if you wish to form the habit of thankfulness, just begin by being thankful—not next year, but tonight; not for some great event or experience, but for whatever has just occurred, whatever has been pleasant, yes, and we did say, for whatever has been painful. You certainly can find some special occasion for thanksgiving this very night. And then go on searching for matter of gratitude, and just continuing to be thankful, hour by hour, day by day. Thus the habit will be formed, by a very law of our nature.

But remember that good habits cannot be maintained without attention. They require a certain self-control, a studious self-constraint. Is not the habit of thankfulness worth taking pains to maintain? The older persons present remember Ole Bull, the celebrated violinist. I once dined in company with him, and in an hour's conversation across the table found him a man of generous soul, full of noble impulses and beautiful enthusiasms, and rich with the experience of wide travel. And I was so much interested in a remark of his which is recorded in the recent biography: "When I stop practicing one day, I see the difference; when I stop two days, my friends see the difference; when I stop a week, everybody sees the difference." Here was a man who had cultivated a wonderful natural gift, by life-long labor, until, as a performer upon the finest of instruments, he was probably the foremost man of his time; and yet he could not afford to stop practicing for a single week, or even for a single day. "They do it for an earthly crown; but we for a heavenly." Christian brethren, shall we shrink from incessant vigilance and perpetual effort to keep up the habit of thankfulness to God?

I see many young persons present this evening. Will not some of you at once begin the thoughtful exercise of continual thankfulness? Will you not think over it, pray over it, labor to establish and maintain so beautiful and blessed a habit? Ah, what a help it will be to you amid all the struggles of youth and all the sorrows of age! And in far-coming years, when you are gray, when the preacher of this hour has long been forgotten, let us hope that you will still be gladly recommending to the young around you the Habit of Thankfulness.

3

HE EVER LIVETH TO INTERCEDE

Wherefore also he is able to save to the uttermost them that draw near unto God through him, seeing he ever liveth to make intercession for them. HEBREWS 7:25

YEARS ago, in the city of Philadelphia, I went to hear an eminent musician. He played with genius and skill some magnificent music, but the pieces were nearly all new to me, and, as often happens in such cases, it required so much effort to comprehend the idea of the piece, that I could but partially enjoy its beauty. At length, upon being loudly applauded, the musician returned, and seating himself at the instrument, struck out in full tones the opening notes of "Home, Sweet Home." I shall never forget while I live the thrill that passed through the audience. I seemed to feel that it was approaching me, seemed to feel when it reached and embraced me. That was a theme all could comprehend, and rich for us all in a thousand delightful suggestions and associations; and, strangers as we were, the hearts of the vast assembly seemed melted into one as we listened to those swelling tones.

My brethren, I wish it might always be so with us when one begins to speak to us of Jesus. There is many a subject of public discourse that well deserves our attention. Especially the topics drawn from the Bible and usually presented from the pulpit are all important and should all be interesting. Whatever pertains to God and his province, to his gracious dealings with man in the past, and his purposes of mercy for the future, whatever to the condition and wants of our race as sinful and immortal, should awaken our minds and impress our hearts. Difficult and mysterious as some of these topics are, they are useful; and if we resist the temptation to wander into speculation or descend into secularity, they will give us pleasure and do us good. But Jesus—it is a theme which all alike can understand, in which all alike are profoundly concerned, a theme associated with all the sweetest recollections of our spiritual life, with all the brightest hopes of our immortal future. Ah! we are perishing and helpless sinners, and it ought to thrill through our very hearts, to link us in living sympathy, and kindle our souls into a glow of love and joy to hear of Jesus, our divine, our loving, our precious Saviour. It ought to be not mere poetry, but the true expression of genuine feeling, when we sing,

> Jesus, I love thy charming name;
> 'Tis music to mine ear;
> Fain would I sound it out so loud
> That earth and heaven might hear.

And my text today treats of Jesus.

The Jewish Christians to whom this Epistle was addressed were strongly urged, both in the way of persecution and persuasion, to apostatize from Christianity, and return to Judaism. Among the arguments employed for this purpose, it was urged that Christianity had no priesthood, no sacrifice or temple, and so was really no religion at all. The inspired writer of this Epistle meets these arguments, and, in fact, turns them into proofs of the superiority of Christianity. Thus, in regard to the priesthood, he shows that Christianity has a priest, a great High Priest, immensely superior to the Levitical priesthood. His office is held forever. He has offered, once for all, the wonderful sacrifice of himself, which is forever sufficient. He has passed through the heavens into the true sanctuary, bearing his own precious, atoning blood. Then Christianity is superior in this, as in other respects, to Judaism, that is, to the Mosaic dispensation if regarded as complete in itself, and designed to be permanent; and so the sacred writer urges his brethren not to apostatize, interspersing everywhere throughout his arguments the most earnest exhortations to hold fast their profession, the most solemn warnings of the guilt and ruin of apostasy. For us as well as for them, grievous is the guilt and hopeless the ruin of abandoning the gospel of Christ, our sole hope of salvation.

One of the points he makes to prove this superiority of Christ and Christianity, is that from which the text is an inference. The Levitical priesthood was held by many persons in succession, "because that by death they were hindered from continuing"; but Jesus, "because he abideth forever, hath his priesthood unchangeable. Wherefore he is able to save to the uttermost them that draw near unto God through him, seeing he ever liveth to make intercession for them." The phrase translated "to the uttermost" signifies "perfectly," "completely"; he can save completely, can complete the salvation of them that come unto God through him. And the thought of the text is that he is able to complete their salvation, because he ever lives to intercede for them.

Perhaps we are accustomed to look too exclusively to the Saviour's atoning death, not dwelling as we should upon the idea of his interceding life. See how the apostle speaks in Romans: "For if, while we were enemies, we were reconciled to God through the death of his Son, much more, being reconciled, we shall be saved by his life." And again: "Christ Jesus that died, yea rather that was raised from the dead, who is at the right hand of God, who also maketh intercession for us." He who loved us and gave himself for us ever liveth to accomplish the objects for which he died; as the mediatorial priest, he is ever interceding for the salvation of them that come unto God through him; as the mediatorial king, having all authority given unto him in heaven and earth, he controls all things so as to carry forward to completion the work of their salvation.

My brethren, it is just such a Saviour that we need. From the first moment when we approach God through him, onward through life, and in a certain just sense onward without end, we continually need God's mercy and grace for the Saviour's sake. If we dwell on this, we shall be better prepared to rejoice that our great High Priest ever lives to intercede for us, and thus can complete our salvation.

1. We are tempted. And what hope have we of conquering temptation, save " through him that loved us"? Remember what our Lord said to his disciples, with regard to the sore temptations that would soon befall them: "Simon, Simon, behold, Satan asked to have you, that he might sift you as wheat; but I made supplication for thee, that thy faith fail not." As Satan is described as seeking permission from that Sovereign Ruler, without whose permission all his might and his malice are powerless, to tempt Job with peculiar trials, in the hope that he could bring him to renounce the Lord, so here as to the disciples: "Satan asked to have you"—and the term, as well as the connection, shows that he was permitted to have them, "that he might sift you as wheat."

Jesus himself is represented by John the Baptist as engaged in a similar process: "Whose fan is in his hand, and he will thoroughly cleanse his threshing-floor, and gather his wheat into the garner; but he will burn up the chaff with unquenchable fire." But how different is the object in the two cases! Satan sifts with the hope of showing that all is really worthless, fit only for destruction. Jesus sifts in order to separate the precious from the vile, and preserve the pure wheat for the garner of heaven. And often what Satan meant as a sifting for evil is overruled by the stronger power so as to be for good.

How was it with Peter? The Saviour said: "But I made supplication for thee, that thy faith fail not"; and though his faith mournfully gave way, it did not utterly give out. I am not excusing Peter at all. We may be sure he never forgave himself. It was a sad and shameful fall; but Jesus had made supplication for him; and how different the result in his case from that of Judas. He, too, was one of those whom Satan obtained to sift them, and the result proved him to be all that Satan could wish. When he saw the consequences of his horrid crime, and had time to reflect upon it, he was sorry; but it was not the tender grief of a truly penitent heart which would have brought him back with humble submission—it was the sorrow of the world that worketh death—it was remorse that drove him headlong into self-destruction. But Peter—when the cock crowed after his third denial of his Lord and that injured one turned and looked upon him—Peter went out and wept bitterly, with the sorrow "that worketh repentance unto salvation," the sorrow of a deeply humble and really loving heart. There was a great change from that time in Peter, for the Lord had prayed for him, and divine grace not only preserved him from utter spiritual ruin, but overruled his own dreadful wickedness to his spiritual good.

Observe with what special emphasis the Saviour's intercession for the tempted is spoken of in this Epistle. The persons therein addressed were, as we have seen, peculiarly and sorely tempted—tempted even to forsake Christianity, through which alone they could find salvation; apart from which "there remaineth no more sacrifice for sins, but a certain fearful expectation of judgment and a fierceness of fire which shall devour the adversary." The Jewish high priest, being taken from among men, "could bear gently with the ignorant and erring, for that he himself also was compassed with infirmity." So our great High Priest took upon him human nature partly for this very reason, that he might sympathize with the tempted, and that we might feel sure he does sympathize. "Wherefore in all things it behooved him to be made like unto his brethren, that he might be a merciful and faithful High Priest in things pertaining to God, to make propitiation for the sins of the people. For in that he himself hath suffered being tempted, as he is able to succor them that are tempted."

It is because of his atoning sacrifice and sympathizing intercession that we are urged to hold fast our profession as Christians, and encouraged to come to God with entire confidence. This is done in words that have been very dear to tempted hearts in every age since the holy man of God spake them as he was moved by the Holy Ghost. "Having, then, a great High Priest who hath passed through the heavens, Jesus, the Son of God, let us hold fast our confession. For we have not a high priest that cannot be touched with the feeling of our infirmities; but one that hath been in all points tempted like as we are, yet without sin. Let us therefore draw near with boldness unto the throne of grace that we may receive mercy, and may find grace to help us in time of need."

Ah! mighty, to the most favored, are the temptations of life. Many belong to all periods; others mark some special season. Many are "common to man"; others belong to some particular condition or calling. "The heart knoweth its own bitterness"; yea, and its own trials, and its own weakness. Be this our support—our Saviour lives, he sympathizes with us, he intercedes for us; let us draw near unto God through him, unto God who has said, "As thy days, so shall thy strength be."

> The soul that on Jesus hath leaned for repose,
> I will not, I will not desert to its foes;
> That soul, though all hell should endeavor to shake,
> I'll never, no never, no never forsake.

2. But many times, sad as is the confession, we yield to temptation, we sin; and "the soul that sinneth, it shall die." Must we then despair? Must the hopes we had cherished be abandoned, and this new sin be the terror of our souls? Listen! The apostle John wrote an Epistle for the express purpose of restraining his brethren from sin; yet he does not cut off those who are conscious they have sinned from the hope of forgiveness and salvation. He says: "My little children, these things write I unto you, that ye may not sin. And if any man sin, we have an Advocate with the Father, Jesus Christ, the righteous; and he is the propitiation for our sins; and not for ours only, but also for the whole world."

Now we know what an advocate was, according to the usages of the Roman law, and is among ourselves, viz.: one who undertakes the management of another's case in court, and pleads his cause. So Jesus is our advocate with the Father. But, as in other cases where spiritual things are illustrated by temporal, the analogy is not perfect; there are differences. Our advocate does not argue that we are innocent, but confessing our guilt, pleads for mercy to us; and he does not present *our* merits as a reason why mercy should be shown us, but *his* merits. "He is the propitiation for our sins." His atoning death does, as it were, render God propitious, or favorable to sinners. Not that God is unwilling to show favor to poor sinners, and only prevailed on to do so by the death and intercession of his Son. Oh no! far from it. "Herein is love," says John in the same Epistle, "not that we loved God, but that he loved us, and sent his Son to be the propitiation for our sins." It was because God loved us, and wanted us to be saved, that he devised this way of saving us. And God is made propitious, favorable to us, not when he is made willing to save, but when it is made right that he should save us, and therefore we need not die, but may have everlasting life.

When a sinner is pardoned, simply for the sake of the atoning and interceding Saviour, there is in that no encouragement to God's creatures to sin, as if it were a little thing and could be readily passed over, but a most solemn and impressive exhibition of the dreadful evil of sin, since it was only through the atonement and intercession of the only-begotten Son of God that any sinner could be forgiven— an exhibition at once of God's love to the perishing, and of his justice, that "will by no means clear the guilty."

Bearing in mind the difference between the pleading of our great advocate and any parallel which human affairs presents, we may look at a story of Grecian history, which has been often used to illustrate the Saviour's intercession. The poet Aeschylus had incurred the displeasure of the Athenians. He was on trial before the great popular tribunal, consisting of many hundreds of citizens, and was about to be condemned. But Aeschylus had a brother, who had lost an arm in battle—in the great battle of Salamis, where the Greeks fought for their existence against the Persian aggressors. This brother came into the court, and did not speak words of entreaty, but letting fall his mantle, he showed the stump of his arm, lost in his country's defense, and there stood until the Athenians relented, and Aeschylus was suffered to go free. So, my brethren, imperfect and unworthy as is the illustration, so we may conceive that when we are about to be condemned, and justly condemned for our sins, our glorious Brother stands up in our behalf, and does not need to speak a word, but only to show where he was wounded on the cross—

> Five bleeding wounds he bears,
>   Received on Calvary;
> They pour effectual prayers,
>   They strongly speak for me;
> "Forgive him, O forgive," they cry,
>   "Nor let that ransomed sinner die!"

Here, then, is hope for us. "If any man sin," much as he ought to deplore it, he need not despair. Our advocate with the Father ever liveth to make intercession for them that come unto God through him, and through him we may find mercy. And here is no encouragement to sin, but the very contrary. If we truly trust in, truly love our interceding Lord, we shall be supremely anxious for his dear sake to turn from sin, to live for him who died for us; yea, who ever lives as our Saviour.

3. This suggests another respect in which is seen our need of our Lord's perpetual intercession. We make such slow progress in attaining holiness—holiness, which is the noblest thing men can aspire to—holiness, "without which no man shall see the Lord." Many a Christian, as he sorrowfully sees how often he yields to temptation, how his character breaks down afresh where he thought it had grown most firm, is at times inclined to think it impossible that he should ever become really holy.

But remember how Jesus prayed the night before his atoning death, "Sanctify them in the truth; thy word is truth." "I pray not that thou shouldest take them out of the world, but that thou shouldest keep them from the evil." Think you that he, who ever lives to intercede for his people, does not still pray this prayer, that they may be sanctified and kept from the evil? Do you doubt that he prays for them still, as he did when on earth? His people's wants have not changed, and as for him, he is "the same yesterday and today and forever." Find me a young man far from his home whose mother used to pray for him when they were together, and try to make him believe that she does not pray for him still. "No, no," he would say, "if she is living, she prays for me."

Brethren, he who prays for us "ever lives." When the Jews gathered at the temple on the great day of atonement, and the high priest went into the holy of holies to pray for the people and himself, did the people doubt whether he was praying? Why, for that very purpose he had withdrawn from their view. So for that very purpose our High Priest has entered "not into a holy place made with hands, like in pattern to the true, but into heaven itself, now to appear before the face of God for us." And do not say that the Jewish high priest was absent but a few minutes, while it is long since Jesus went away. On the scale of the ages it is but a little while since he entered the heavenly sanctuary, having "been once offered to bear the sins of many," and any moment he may "appear a second time apart from sin unto salvation." Let us be sure that while absent he perpetually carries on his work of intercession.

Think of him, then, as still praying, "Sanctify them in the truth. Keep them from the evil." In all our disheartening failures to keep

good resolutions, even when we may be tempted to think it scarce
worth while for us to try to be holy, let us remember that Jesus prays
for us, and, "forgetting the things which are behind, and reaching
forth unto those things which are before, let us press toward the
mark." Ah! brethren, though it might often seem to us the bitterest
irony now for a man to call you and me the saints of the Lord, yet,
if indeed we are in Christ, and thus are new creatures, we have but
to trust in his intercession for the sanctifying Spirit, and earnestly
strive to "grow in grace," and we shall make progress; yea, sadly
imperfect as is now our conformity to the Saviour's beautiful image,
"we know that when he shall appear we shall be like him, for we shall
see him as he is." O burdened spirit, crying, "Wretched man that I
am, who shall deliver me from the body of this death?" be sure to
add, "I thank God, through Jesus Christ our Lord." The Saviour will
continue to intercede, the Spirit will help your infirmities, and you
shall at last be pure from sin, and safe from temptation to sin, a saint
of the Lord forever.

4. When we are in sorrow it is a blessed thing that Jesus ever
lives to pray for us. He was himself while on earth, "a man of
sorrows, and acquainted with grief." And he showed the truest, tenderest sympathy with the sorrows of others. Who does not think at
once of that touching scene at Bethany? "Jesus wept," in affection
for the departed, in sympathy with the bereaved. And presently,
standing by the tomb, he said, "Father, I thank thee that thou hast
heard me." Then he had been praying, asking that he might be able
to raise Lazarus from the dead. We do not expect him now to pray
that miracles may be wrought in behalf of the bereaved. We do not
expect him now to give back the buried brother to his sisters, or to
the widowed mother her only son. But shall it not be a consolation
to us all in our afflictions, to feel assured that he now intercedes for
us; that now, too, the Father hears him, and that by the gracious
influences of the Holy Ghost, the Comforter, this affliction shall
work for us glory? And though we cannot now see his tears, nor hear
his loving voice, as did the mourners at Bethany, neither do we need
to send a messenger many miles, and wait, day after day, and go
forth into the suburbs to meet him; he is everywhere alike near, and
ever ready to pray for us to his Father and our Father, to his God
and our God.

5. When we come to die—he is "alive forevermore." One of his
servants, when near to death, saw "heaven opened, and the Son of
Man standing on the right hand of God," where he represents and intercedes for his people. And so in departing he committed his spirit

to him, as now exalted and glorious and ready to receive it. And so, amid all the cruel injustice and suffering, he was calm and forgiving. And so, though they were stoning him to death, "he fell asleep." Oh, whenever you are called to die, brother, and however, whether among loving friends in your pleasant home, or far away in loneliness and want, whether with ample forewarning or in the suddenness of a moment, think of your interceding Saviour standing on the right hand of God, and say, "Lord Jesus, receive my spirit," and you too shall fall asleep.

6. Even this is not the end of his work for his people. There shall be a "redemption of the body." Many have been sad during the time of war, because the bodies of their loved ones lie so far away, lie perhaps undistinguished among the huge masses of the unnamed dead. But he who receives the departing spirit to himself will also care for the mouldering body. His resurrection is a pledge of the glorious resurrection of his people. "If we believe that Jesus died and rose again, even so them also who through Jesus have fallen asleep, will God bring with him." "Who shall fashion anew the body of our humiliation, that it may be conformed to the body of his glory." Then, the spirit reunited with the risen and glorified body, "so shall we ever be with the Lord."

And he who saved them will be ever living to keep them safe, unto all eternity.

My friends, how shall we think of Jesus? What conception shall we cherish of him whom "having not seen, we love," who ever liveth to intercede for us? Many centuries ago, on the eastern slope of Mount Olivet, toward Bethany, twelve men stood together, one talking to the others. Presently he lifted up his hands and blessed them; and with hands still uplifted, and words of blessing still lingering on his lips, he was parted from them and rose toward heaven, till a cloud received him out of sight. Years passed, and one of the eleven was an exile on a lonely island. It was the Lord's day, and he was in the Spirit. Hearing behind him a mighty voice that seemed to call him, he turned, and lo! one like unto the Son of Man—it was the Saviour who had parted from him long years before. He was arrayed in robes of majesty, and girt about with a golden girdle; his whole head shone white as snow with celestial glory; his eyes were as a flame of fire; and his feet like unto burnished brass, as if it had been refined in a furnace; and his voice as the voice of many waters; and his countenance as the sun shineth in his strength. Yes, the feet that once wearily trod the dusty roads of Judea now shone like molten brass. The eyes that were full of tears as he gazed upon doomed Jerusalem now gleamed as a flame of fire. The countenance that writhed in agony as he lay prostrate on his face in the garden, that was streaked with the blood that fell from his thorn-pierced brow, was now as the sun shineth in his strength. And the voice as the voice of many waters—it was the same voice that in gentleness and love had so often encouraged the sinful and sorrowing to draw near— it is the same voice that now calls us to come unto God through him, and declares that he is able to save us completely, since he ever lives to intercede for us.

O my hearer, slight all the sounds of earth, all the voices of the universe; be deaf to the thunder's mighty tones, and stand careless amid "the wreck of matter and the crush of worlds"—but oh, slight not the loving voice of Jesus.

4

WORSHIP

God is a Spirit, and they that worship him must worship him
in spirit and truth. JOHN 4:24

JESUS was tired. The little that we know of the history just before
yet enables us to see cause why he should have been tired.

He had been, for long months, engaged in active efforts to save
men's souls—to lift men out of their sluggishness and worldliness
toward God. That is hard work for mind and heart. And he had been
at work among many who were jealous. The disciples of John were
some of them envious that their master was decreasing and another
was increasing, though John said it was right and good; and when
the Pharisees heard that Jesus was now making and baptizing more
disciples than John, they were jealous. They made it needful that he
should withdraw from Judea, as so often during his brief ministry
he had to withdraw from the jealousy of his enemies or the fanaticism
of his friends, and seek a new field. Worn out and perhaps sad at
heart, the Redeemer sat alone by Jacob's well.

Our artists owe us yet two companion pictures—the one of Jesus,
as the disciples saw him when they turned back to look, on their way
to buy food, as he sat and rested, leaning with limbs relaxed, with
face weary, yet gentle; and the other of Jesus as they found him when
they came back, sitting up now with an animated look on his face,
busily, eagerly talking.

Ah! there was an opening to do good, and he who "went about
doing good" would give up even his needed rest, and often did, to do
good to the least and the lowest. The disciples wondered not that he
was ready to do good; they had seen that often already. They wondered that he was talking with a woman, for that was contrary to the
dignity of a man according to the ideas of that time and country—
to be seen talking with a woman in public. They wondered; they
knew not yet what manner of spirit they were of—that they had to
deal with high-saving truths that break through all weak convention-
alities.

They would have wondered more if they had known what he knew full well—that it was a woman of bad character; and yet he saw in her potencies for good, and he did win her that day to faith in the Messiah who had come, and sent her forth to tell others to come and see "a man who had told her all things whatsoever she did."

But she shrank in the process. Beautiful and wonderful it is to see how admirably our Lord led the casual conversation with a stranger so as to introduce the profoundest spiritual truths.

My Christian friends, let me not fail to point your attention to this. I know no art of social life more needful to be cultivated in our time and country than the art of skillfully introducing religion into general conversation. It is a difficult task. It requires tact and skill to do this in such a way as to accomplish much good and no harm; but it is worth all your efforts. Old and young, men and women, yea—shall I say it?—especially young ladies, who are Christians, with that control which young ladies have in our American society, need to cultivate few things so much as just that power which the Redeemer possessed. Oh! beautiful, blessed example of Jesus! How it shines more and more as we study and strive to imitate it! And not only did he lead on toward religious truth, but he knew how, in a quiet, skillful way, to awaken her consciousness to a realization of her sinfulness, so that she might come near to spiritual truth. She shrank from it, I said, as people will often shrink from us when we try to bring truth home to their souls. She shrank, and while not wishing to turn the conversation entirely away from religious things, she would turn it away to something not so uncomfortably close, and so she asked him about a great question much discussed.

"Sir, I perceive that thou art a prophet. Our fathers did worship in this mountain," and right up the steep slopes of Mount Gerizim she would point to the mount high above them, where were the ruins of the old temple of the Samaritans, destroyed a century and a half before. "Our fathers worshipped in this mountain; and ye say that in Jerusalem is the place where men ought to worship. O prophet, which is it?" Again the Redeemer, while he answers her question, will turn it away from all matters of form and outward service, and strike deep by a blow into the spiritual heart of things. "Woman, believe me, the hour is coming, when neither in this mountain nor in Jerusalem shall ye worship the Father." He will not fail to imply in passing that Jerusalem had been the right place. "Ye worship that which ye know not. We worship that which we know, for salvation is from the Jews"— he only mentions that in passing—"but the hour cometh and now is, when the true worshippers shall worship the Father in spirit and truth, for such doth the Father seek to be his worshippers."

Only spiritual worship will be acceptable to God; this is what he seeks, and, more than that, this is what the very nature of the case requires. "God is a spirit, and they that worship him must worship him in spirit and truth."

I wish to speak of the worship of God, and I shall ask two very simple questions about it, and try to some extent to answer each of them.

Why should we worship God? How should we worship God?

I. A man might well draw back and fear to say one word as to reasons why we should worship God. Oh! how high, and wide, and deep, that theme! Yet it may be useful just to remind you of some things included in these expressions. Why should we worship God? Because it is due to him; and because it is good for us.

1. That we should render to God worship is due to him. My dear friends, if we were but unconcerned spectators of the glorious God and his wonderful works, it should draw from our hearts admiration, adoration, and loving worship. The German philosopher, Kant, probably the greatest philosopher of modern times, said: "There are two things that always awaken in me, when I contemplate them, the sentiment of the sublime. They are the starry heavens and the moral nature of man." Oh! God made them both, and all there is of the sublime in either or in both is but a dim, poor reflection of the glory of him who made them. Whatever there is in this world that is suited to lift up men's souls at all ought to lift them toward God.

Robert Hall said that the idea of God subordinates to itself all that is great, borrows splendor from all that is fair, and sits enthroned on the riches of the universe. More than that is true. I repeat, all that exalts our souls ought to lift them up toward God. Especially ought we to adore the holiness of God.

O sinful human beings, still you know that holiness is the crown of existence. There is not a human heart that does not somehow, sometimes love goodness. Find me the most wicked man in all your great city, and there are times when that man admires goodness. Yea, I fancy that there are times when he hopes that somehow or other he may yet be good himself. When a man we love has died, we are prone to exaggerate in our funeral discourse, in our inscriptions on tombstones and the like—to exaggerate what? We seldom exaggerate much in speaking of a man's talents, or learning, or possessions, or influence, but we are always ready to exaggerate his goodness. We want to make the best of the man in that solemn hour. We feel that goodness is the great thing for a human being when he has gone out of our view into the world unseen. What is it that the Scriptures teach us in one of the great themes of the high worship of God, where worship is perfect? Long ago a prophet saw the Lord seated high on a throne in the temple, with flowing robes of majesty, and on either side adoring seraphs did bend and worship, and oh! what was it that was the theme of their worship? Was it God's power? Was it God's wisdom? You know what they said—"Holy, holy, holy, is the Lord of hosts. The whole earth is full of his glory." And there do come times, O my friends, to you and me, though we lift not holy hands, when we want to adore the holiness of God.

Then think of his love and mercy! If you were only unconcerned spectators I said—think of his love and mercy! He hates sin. We know how to hate sin as the holy God must hate it. And yet he loves the sinner! How he yearns over the sinful! How he longs to save him! Oh, heaven and earth, God so loved the world that he gave his only begotten Son, that whosoever will have it so, might through him be saved.

I know where that great provision, that mighty mercy, is adored. I know from God's Word that those high and glorious ones, who know far more than we do of the glorious attributes of the Creator and the wide wonders of his works, when they have sung their highest song of praise for God's character and for creation, will then strike a higher note as they sing the praises of redemption, for holiness and redemption are the great themes which the Scriptures make known to us of the worship in heaven. John saw in his vision how the four living creatures, representing the powers of nature, and the four and twenty elders, representing the saved of God, bowed in worship, and how a wide and encircling host of angels caught the sound, and how it spread wider still, till in all the universe it rolls, "Salvation and honor and glory and power be unto him that sitteth on the throne and unto the Lamb forever and ever."

Holiness and redemption! We ought to adore if we had nothing to do with it, for we have a moral nature to appreciate it. And oh! are we unconcerned spectators? That most wonderful manifestation of God's mercy and love has been made toward us. And, if the angels find their highest theme of praise in what the gracious God has done for us, how should we feel about it? Yea, there is a sense in which, amid the infirmities of earth, we can pay God a worship that the angels cannot themselves offer.

> Earth has a joy unknown in heaven;
> The new-born bliss of sins forgiven.

And sinful beings out of grateful hearts for sins forgiven may strike a note of praise to God that shall pierce through all the high anthems of the skies and enter into the ear of the Lord God of Hosts.

2. Moreover, we should worship God, not only because it is due to him, but because it is good for us. Only the worship of God can satisfy, O my friends, the highest and noblest aspirations of our natures.

When anything lifts us up, then we want God as the climax of our exalted thought, and our thought itself is imperfect without it. If you will look, as I looked this morning, in the early light, upon the glory of the autumn woods, faded now, yet still bright and beautiful; if you gaze upon the splendor of the nightly skies; if you stand in awe before the great mountains, snow-clad and towering; if you go and gaze in the silence of night upon the rush of your own imperial river, or stand by the seashore, and hear the mighty waters rolling evermore, there swells in the breast something that wants God for its crown and for its completeness. There are aspirations in these strange natures of ours that only God can satisfy. Our thinking is a mutilated fragment without God, and our hearts can never rest unless they rest in God.

And worship, oh, how it can soothe! Yea, sometimes worship alone can soothe our sorrows and our anxieties. There come times with all of us when everything else does fail us; there come times when we go to speak with sorrowing friends and feel that all our themes are weak and vain. You, wicked man yonder—you have gone sometimes to visit a friend that was in great distress, who had lost a dear child or husband, or wife; and as you have sat down by your friend and wanted to say something comforting, you have felt that everything else was vain but to point the poor sorrowing heart to God; and you felt ashamed of yourself that you did not dare to do that. How often have devout hearts found comfort in sorrow, found support in anxiety, by the worship of God; by the thought of submission to God and trust in God; a belief that God knows what he is doing; that God sees the end from the beginning; that God makes "all things work together for good to those that love him!"

Furthermore, the worship of God nourishes the deepest root of morality—individual and social. Morality cannot live upon mere ideas of expediency and utility. The root of morality is the sentiment of moral obligation. What does it mean when your little child first begins to say "I ought to do this" and "I ought not to do that"? What does it mean? "I ought." The beasts around us are some of them very intelligent. They seem to think in a crude fashion. They seem to reason in a rudimentary way. Our intellect is not peculiar to us. They have something of it, but they show no sign of having the rudiments of the notion that "I ought" and "I ought not." It is the glory of man. It makes him in the image of the spiritual one that made him. And what is to nourish and keep alive and make strong that sentiment of moral obligation in our souls? It is the recognition of the fact that there is a God who gave us this high, moral, spiritual being; who made us for himself; to whom we belong. It is our worship of him which nourishes in us the highest and best. How can a man tell the reasons why we should worship God? They are as high as heaven, as wide as the world, as vast as the universe; all existence and all conception—everything is a reason why we should worship God.

II. How much should we worship God? I wish here to speak only of that line of thought which the text presents, How shall we worship God with spiritual worship?

The spiritual worship the text points out to us is essentially independent of localities. Time was when it was not so: when the best worship that was to be expected in the world depended upon holy places and impressive rites. In the childhood of the race these ideas were necessary, but Christianity came as the maturity of revealed religion, and declared that those ideas should prevail no longer; that true Christian spiritual worship is essentially independent of localities.

My friends, under the Christian system you cannot make holy places; you cannot make a holy house. We speak very naturally and properly enough, if with due limitation, in the language of the Old Testament, about our places of worship, but we ought to remember constantly the limitations. You cannot consecrate a building in the light of Christianity. You can dedicate the building, you can set it apart to be used only for the worship of God; but you cannot make the house a holy house; it is an idea foreign to the intense spirituality which Jesus has taught us belongs to the Christian idea of worship.

Why, then, one might say, why should we have houses of worship? Not merely because if there is to be the worship of assemblies at all, with all the strange power that sympathy gives to aggregated worship, then there must be places of assembly; but because these soon become associated with the solemn worship we hold in them and sacred by their associations, and if we do not disturb those associations, if from the places where we are wont to hold solemn worship, we keep carefully away all that tends to violate those associations, they grow in power upon us; they do not make the place holy, but they make it easier by force of association and of beneficent habit for us to have holy thoughts and to pay holy worship in the place where we have often paid it before. So we can see why it is fit to set apart places of worship, houses of worship for God, though they be not in themselves holy, though spiritual worship is independent of locality.

Let us rise to a broader view of the matter. Spiritual worship must subordinate all these externals.

Can you listen a few minutes while I offer a plain, unadorned, unimpassioned statement about this really practical matter, surely suitable to our circumstances, worthy to be discussed; for there are many extremes about it among men, and though you may not go with my thought, it may help you to think the matter through for yourself. I say, then, on the one hand, spiritual worship must have its externals. For while we are spiritual, like God, we are something else also. We have a material nature, and we are all closely linked and interdependent and acting upon each other continually. It is idle, then, to think that our worship will be all that it is capable of becoming if we try to keep it exclusively spiritual and give it no outward expression at all. When you try to pray in private by your own bedside, alone with your beating heart and your God, you mistake if you try to pray without couching your thought and feeling in words. We need the force of expression, though we utter not the words. We need to have the words in order to give clearness and form to our thought and our sentiment; and it is good, even when alone, in low, solemn tones to speak aloud one's private prayer, for that seems somehow, by a law of our nature, to make deeper the feeling which we thus outwardly express; and if we do so even in private prayer, how much more is it necessarily true in public worship!

We must have expression then for our worship, that there may be sympathy—expression that shall awaken and command sympathy. We must use the language of imagination and passion as in the Scriptures. The Scriptures are full of the language of imagination and passion—language that is meant to stir the souls of men. And when we sing—sing in the simplest and plainest way, if you please— we are yet striving to use that as one of the externals of spiritual worship. We need it. We must have externals. Why, then—a man might ask, and men often have asked—why not have anything and everything that will contribute at all to help the expression and cherish the devout feeling? Why not have everything in architecture, everything in painting and statuary, everything in special garments, in solemn processions, in significant posture? Why not anything and everything that may at all help as an external expression of devout feeling?

Let us consider this, I pray you. I said spiritual worship must have its externals, and now I repeat that it must subordinate those externals; whatever externals it cannot subordinate it must discard, and the externals it does employ it must employ heedfully. There are some things that awaken in some men a sort of fictitious, quasi-devout feeling, which you never would think of recommending as aids to devotion. Some persons when they use opium have a dreamy sort of devoutness, and some persons, even when they become drunk, show a morbid sort of religion. Yet who would think of saying that these are acts that help to devotion?

But there are feelings that are right in themselves and noble in their place that do in some cases help to promote devotional feeling. The husband and wife, when they bow down with their children by their sides to pray together, and then, rising up, look lovingly into each other's eyes, find their devout feeling toward God heightened by their love for each other and their children. I can fancy that the young man and maiden who both fear God and have learned to love each other may sometimes feel their devout sentiments truly heightened by this new, strange and beautiful affection which they have learned to feel for each other. That is so sometimes, and yet everybody sees that to recommend that as an avowed and systematic thing to be used as a help to devotion would be out of the question. Not everything, then, that may promote devotion is to be regularly used for this purpose.

There are some things that look as if they were necessary, are very often recommended as helpful, and often employed as helps, that turn out to be dangerous and erroneous. Why can't we use pictures and statuary as helps to devotion? Why can't we employ them as proper means of making the thought of our Saviour near and dear to us? Well, in all the ages of the world, the heathen have tried this. An educated young Hindu, some years ago, educated in England, wrote an essay in which he complained bitterly that the Hindus were accused of worshiping images, and quoted Cowper's beautiful poem entitled, "My Mother's Picture":

O, that those lips and language!
Years have passed since thee I saw.

And he says, the picture of the poet's mother brought close and made real the thought of one long dead. That is the way, he said, that we use images. But that is not the way that the great mass of men use images in worship. They have often meant that at the outset; but how soon it degenerated and was degraded, and these things that were meant as helps to worship dragged down the aspirations of human hearts, instead of lifting them up! But, it seems to me, if I were to employ such helps in our time, persuading myself that they would be good, that I should feel it was wise to go back to the old ten commandments that we teach our children to repeat, and cut out the second commandment, that expressly forbids the use of graven images, because it necessarily leads to idolatry. I should cut that out. You can inquire, if you are curious to do so—and I say it in no unkindness—you can inquire whether those Christians in our own time and country who employ pictures and statuary today as helps to devotion have mutilated the ten commandments. They were obliged to leave out that which their little children would say was forbidding what they do.

Aye, the world has tried that experiment widely and in every way, and it is found that though you might think that pictures and statuary would be helps to devotion, they turn out to be hurtful. They may help a few; they harm many. They may do a little good; they do much evil.

But there are some of these things which we must have to some extent—church buildings, architecture, music, cultivated eloquence. How about these? We are obliged to have these. We must have the rude and coarse, if we have not the refined and elegant; and just what we may have in this respect—why, it depends, of course, upon what we have been accustomed to in our homes, our places of public assembly, our halls of justice. That which is natural, needful and good for some would utterly distract the attention of others. Take a man from the most ignorant rural region, utterly unused to such things, and place him in this house next Sunday morning, and his attention would be utterly distracted by the architectural beauties of the place and the strange power of the music, and he would be scarcely able to have any other thought. These things would be hurtful to him; but to those who have been used to them and who, in their own houses, have been accustomed to elegance and beauty, or in the homes of others they sometimes enter, or in the great places of public assembly in the cities where they live, these things need not be hurtful to them. They may be helpful to them. Ah, my friends, they need to be used by us all with caution and with earnest efforts to make them helpful to devotion, or they will drag down our attention to themselves. Often it is so. You go home with your children, talking only about the beauty of your house of worship or the beauty of the music, and how soon your children will come to think and feel that

that is all there is to come to church for, and how many there are
who do thus think and feel.

It is easy to talk nonsense on the subject of church music. It is
very difficult to talk wisely. But I think we sometimes forget in our
time that there is a distinction between secular and sacred music.
I have seen places where they did not seem to know there was such
a distinction. They seem to have obliterated it by using so much
purely secular music in sacred worship. It is a distinction not easy to
define, I know, but easy enough to comprehend on the part of one
who is cultivated and has an ear for music and a heart for devotion.
It is a distinction that ought always to be heedfully regarded. Beautiful church music, I delight in; but we must learn to use it as a help
to devotion, or else we are using it wrong, and it will do us harm.
We must not only cultivate the use and enjoyment of artistic music
for the sake of enjoyment, but what is far more than enjoyment,
we must cultivate the power of making it a help to religious worship.
We must learn to do that, or we must refuse to have it.

My friends, you should rejoice in the high privileges of cultivated society and refined homes, beautiful places of worship,
glorious sounds of music and a lofty style of eloquence; but there is
danger for you. I have heard people say, "I don't believe in the
religion of those who work themselves into a mere animal excitement. They sway their bodies, and parade around the room, and shake
hands, and shout, and embrace each other, and work up mere
animal excitement; but there is no religion in that." Oh, you child
of culture! Go to your beautiful place of worship, with its dim religious light, its pealing organ, its highly cultivated gentleman,
trained in elegant literature to speak in a beautiful style, as he ought
to do, and you may have excited in you a mere aesthetic sentiment
which may have no more real worship in it than "animal excitement."
But, thank God! there may be genuine religion in both.

There is danger there, but my friends there is always danger and
we must learn to discard that which we cannot subordinate to spiritual
worship. I pray you, then, do not go to asking people to come just to
see your beautiful house of worship or to listen to your noble music.
Some will come for that reason alone, and you cannot help it. But do
not encourage such a thought. Talk about worship. Talk about these
externals as helps to the solemn worship of God. Try to take that
view of it. Try to make other people take that view of it. Try to
speak of worship for its own sake and not for the sake of the
aesthetic gratification it may give.

Still another thought on spiritual worship. I think that in most of

our churches—our churches that have no set ritual, no fixed form
of worship—there is a disposition to underrate the importance of
public worship; to think only of the preaching. I notice that in those
churches, not only our own, but those like it that have no special
form of worship, they always give notice for preaching and not for
worship, they only talk about the preacher and not the worship. They
seem to think it makes little difference if they are too late for worship,
provided they are there in time for the sermon. I notice that many
preachers seem to give their whole thought to their sermon, and think
nothing of preparing themselves for that high task, that solemn, re-
sponsible undertaking, to try to lift up the hearts of a great assembly
in prayer to God.

What I wish to say is, wherever that may be true, let us consider
whether we ought not to take more interest in our worship, in the
reading of God's word for devotional impression, in solemn, sacred
song and in humble prayer to God, in which we wish the hearts of
the whole assembly to rise and melt together. It is true that we must
have a care how we cultivate variety here, for the hearts of men
seem to take delight in something of routine in their worship; they
are rested if they know what comes next; they are harassed often if
they are frequently disappointed and something quite unexpected
comes in. We must keep our variety within limits, but within limits
we must cultivate variety.

I believe there should be more attention paid to making our
worship varied in its interest than is usually the case; and then, O
my brethren, something far more important for the preacher and
people is this—we must put heart into our worship. We must not care
merely to hear a man preach. I do not wish you to think less of
preaching, but more of the other. We must put heart into our worship.
Even the sermon is a two-sided thing—one side of it is part of our
worship so far as it causes devotional feeling and lifts up the heart
toward God, though on its other side of instruction and exhortation
it is distinct from worship.

Now, I say we must put heart in our worship. Do not venture to
come to this beautiful place of worship, or whatever place of
worship you attend, and just sit languidly down to see if the choir can
stir you or to see if the preacher can stir you. Oh! stir up your own
souls. It is your solemn duty when you go to engage with others in
the worship of God—it is your duty to yourself, it is your duty to
others, it is your duty to the pastor who wishes to lead your worship,
it is your duty to God, who wants the hearts of men, and who will have
nothing but their hearts. I know how we feel. Worn by a week's toil,

What do our eyes see when we come to worship?

languid on the Lord's day through lack of our customary excitement, we go to take our places, jaded and dull, and we are tempted to think, "Now I will see whether the services can make any impression on me; whether the preacher can get hold of me—I hope they may," and we sit passive to wait and see. Oh, let us not dare thus to deal with the solemnity of the worship of God.

My brethren, if we learn to worship aright, there will be beautiful and blessed consequences. It will bring far more of good to our own souls. It will make worship far more impressive to our children. Have you not observed that it is getting to be one of the questions of our day how the Sunday school children are to be drawn to our public worship. We are often told that the preacher must try to make his sermon more attractive to children, and so he must. But let us also make our worship more impressive, and make our children feel that it is their duty to worship God, and try to bring them under the influence of this worship. I heard in Washington one of the foremost Sunday school laborers of this country, a Methodist minister, make this statement in private: He said: "Of late I have been telling the people everywhere, if your children cannot do both, cannot go to Sunday school and go to the public worship also, keep them away from the Sunday school, for they must go to the public worship." You may call that an extravagant statement. I am not sure that it is extravagant, but I am sure of this, that we need not merely to try to make our preaching attract children, but to try to make the worship so solemn, so real, so genuine, so earnest, that those strange little earnest hearts of our children will feel that there is something there that strikes to their souls.

And if you have true, fervent worship of God, the stranger that comes into your place of worship will feel it too. Have you not noticed when you go into some houses how quickly you perceive that you are in an atmosphere of hospitality and kindness? There may be no parade, no speech-making. Yet in some places you may feel it, you feel it in the atmosphere, you feel it at once in your soul; you see a place where they are kindly and loving. So it ought to be, that when a man comes into your place of worship he shall very soon feel a something that pervades the atmosphere he breathes, from the look of the people, from the solemn stillness, from the unaffected earnestness he shall feel that these people are genuine, solemn worshipers of God. When he feels that, he will conclude that God is with you of a truth and there will be power to move his soul in your solemn worship.

Now, my brethren, in this beautiful house which you have built for the worship of God, and are now dedicating to his worship, oh, may there be much real spiritual worship. When your hearts are full sometimes and you come and try to throw your souls into God's worship, may you be moved and melted; when you are sorely tempted sometimes and coming to the house of God, try to lift your heart to him in prayer, may you get good from the wise and loving words of the man you love to see stand before you as your pastor.

As your children grow up by your side and learn to delight with you in coming to the house of God in company, oh, may you be permitted to see more and more of them gladly coming to tell what great things God has done for their souls, and gladly coming to put on Christ by baptism. And not only the children of your households, but strangers within your gates.

Yes, and when the young of your households begin to link those households more closely than ever together, and on the bright bridal day the brilliant procession comes sweeping up the aisle and all men's hearts are glad; may they always come reverently in the fear of the God they have here learned to worship. And O mortal men and women, who have united to build high and glorious piles that will stand when you are gone, when in the hour of your departure from the works of your hands, and from the worship that you loved on earth, and slow and solemn up the aisle they bear the casket that holds all that is left to earth of you, and behind come sad-faced men and sobbing women, and while the solemn music sounds through all these vaults and your pastor rises, struggling to control his own sorrow for the death of one he loved so well—oh, may it be true, in that hour which is coming—may you begin from this night so to live that it shall then be true, that the mourners of that hour may sorrow here, not as those who have no hope, and that the men and women who honor you, and have gathered to pay honor to your memory, may feel like saying in simple sincerity as they look upon your coffin, "The memory of the just is blessed; let me die the death of the righteous and let my last end be like his." Oh, begin today, God help you to begin from this hour of entrance into your new place of worship so to live that all this may be true when you pass away.

5

ONE JESUS

And of one Jesus, which was dead, whom Paul affirmed to
be alive. ACTS 25:19

A NEW military governor had come to Caesarea. The people knew
well enough that it was important for all those who had anything
to do, especially with the government, to make the acquaintance of
this man and try to gain his favor. For in all such cases the character
and good will of the ruler was a matter of consequence. Among the
persons who hurried to Caesarea to meet the governor Festus was a
native ruler, a young man named Herod Agrippa.

He was a great grandson of the celebrated Herod the Great, and
was at that time allowed by the Romans to be a king, subject to
them, over the northeastern portion of his ancestor's dominions.
Agrippa came and spent a number of days at Caesarea. He had been
educated in Rome, but as there were no newspapers, there would
be much information which Agrippa could obtain from the governor
respecting the state of society and the gossip of the capital.

On the other hand there would much that Agrippa could tell the
governor about the curious people he had come to rule over, a people
well known over the world for their excitability and extraordinary
stubbornness, a people hard to govern and hard to understand.
And so the days went on with varied talk and counsel and feasts and
baths and theater and gladiators, and all the apparatus of Roman
luxury which Herod the Great had gathered in his capital city of
Caesarea.

After Agrippa had been there many days, we are told it occurred
to Festus—possibly he was coming to be a little at a loss for new
subjects of conversation—to mention to the young king a singular
prisoner whom his predecessor Felix had left there in prison, a man
named Paul, whom he found to be exceedingly unpopular with the
Jewish rulers though he could not exactly understand why. For when
the Jewish rulers were summoned before him according to the Roman

custom, he found they had no accusation to make against the man—
no civil offense—but they had certain questions of their own superstition and about one Jesus who was dead, whom Paul affirmed to
be alive. One Jesus. How little did the Roman governor dream that
as a fly preserved in amber he was going to be remembered in the
world's history simply because of his connections with Paul the
prisoner and with this Jesus!

Things have changed since then. The long progress of what we
call the Christian centuries has brought its changes and we live in
what calls itself a Christian land after Jesus Christ. And yet, O my
friends, it is very sorrowful to think how many there are, even in this
so-called Christian land, who seem to care very little more about
Jesus Christ than poor Festus did. Busy, some of them are with
philosophical thought, and some with schemes of statesmanship, and
some with the charms of literature, busy with the harassing pursuits
of life, with its perplexing cares, with its bewildering pleasures, busy
with everything else and hardly ever a thought at all of Jesus. What
I wish to say is simply this: there is no one who has a right to think
lightly of Jesus, and I wish to offer some reasons why that is so.

In the first place, Jesus is the most important personage in human
history. The obscure and insignificant one, of whom Festus spoke so
carelessly, has founded this world's most wonderful empire. The
carpenter of Nazareth is a king of men. You will remember what
Napoleon said, and those words have often been repeated, as he
spoke to one of his friends during life, "Alexander, Caesar, Charle-
magne, and myself founded empires, but they were force, upheld
by force, and when the force was withdrawn, how soon they all
mouldered away. Jesus Christ has founded an empire of love, and it
lives through all the ages, and nothing seems able to destroy it."
Yea, from him went forth the influences which have given to what
we call Christian civilization, its highest dignity, its truest power.
Much we have derived, no doubt, from Grecian literature and art, and
Roman law, and something from our Gothic ancestors, but the chief
power in Christian civilization comes from that Jesus.

Yea, the men nowadays who fancy they can do without Christianity, who prate that they have risen above Christianity to a higher plane
than it has reached, seem not to know that all the elevated ethical
conceptions and sentiments of which they boast and which they suppose make them independent are but the result of this same Christianity which they disdain. They are like a silly schoolboy who has but half
learned a few of the teacher's lessons, and then fancies he knows more
than the teacher and can henceforth do without him. Yea, the thought-

ful world is coming to see somewhat more clearly that Jesus is the center of the world's history. Bossuet made that remark, and it has often been repeated: that the cross of Jesus Christ is the center of the world's history. All lines of preceding events seem to converge to that cross, and from it diverge all the great events of the world's subsequent history.

It is a kindred thought to say that Jesus is the center of the Scriptures. Everything in the Old Testament points forward to him: everything in the New Testament proceeds forth from him. You cannot understand the history of the Old Testament, if you think of it merely as a history of Israel. It is a history of redemption, that is its characteristic idea, and in Jesus Christ it has found its consummation, its climax, its completeness. Jesus is for us indeed the pledge of the divine authority of the Old Testament. Does a man say, "How do you know that what we call the Old Testament is from God?" I answer, the Jews were just as familiar in our Lord's time, as we are, with the phrase "The Scriptures." "The Scriptures," used so often in the Old Testament, and we know from Jewish chronicles that what they meant by Scripture was the Hebrew books which we call the Old Testament, and this selfsame scripture Jesus declares is from God and cannot be broken. I stand hearing his testimony to its authority and am content.

Men rise up in every successive age and say science has at last discovered—they seem to imagine that science will never make any discoveries after their age—science has at last discovered certain facts which are incompatible with the Old Testament. Jesus declares the Scriptures cannot be broken, and I believe that whenever physical science has truly interpreted the works of God, which is only partially done as yet as every thoughtful man knows, and philological science has rightly interpreted the Word of God, that people who are prepared for it will see that there is no conflict. In the meantime the conflict we hear so much about grows out of the hasty conclusions of those who but partially understand God's workings, and still more partially understand God's providence. Jesus says that the Scripture is God's Word and cannot be broken and I am content. I am dependent upon no man's knowledge. Let knowledge come and welcome, only when it comes to be knowledge then we will turn to God's Word and study the passages and we will see about the so-called conflict.

So trusting in Jesus, we make sure concerning the miracles he wrought. People say, and it is not an unnatural question, how do you know but that the persons who witnessed the miracles of Christ were deluded, not to say deceivers? Well, much might be said about their character, and about the fact that both friend and foe united in bearing witness to these things, but apart from all these Jesus himself declared, over and again, that he did work these miracles by the favor of God, and who is going to say that he was deluded and who is going to say that he was a deceiver? His character bears testimony to the reality of his miracles, and his character and his miracles like two sides of an arch holding each other up, support the whole fabric of Christianity. Against his character, all human opposition breaks and is shattered like surf against a rock. The few men that have ventured to try to say something against the character of Jesus, their tongues have not been palsied but their words have been manifestly weak and vain.

It is not strange that the history of Jesus himself, the center of Scripture, has come to be the great subject of inquiry among the friends and foes of the Christian religion. In our time you have all noticed how many books have been written in the last generation on the life of Christ—the like of it never seen before—in Germany and France, in England and America. There is a work about to be published now in this city about the life of Christ, more elaborate in some respects than any before published. And why so much of this? Because the world is beginning to feel that Jesus is the center of Scripture; that Christianity is in the world and the character and the work of Jesus himself. The men who question its power and who deny its authority are coming to see that Christianity is in the world though, and has been a mighty power in the world, and though often grievously perverted and misdirected, is on the whole a beneficent and blessed power, and they have got to account for it. That means study the history of Jesus.

Yea, Jesus is the whole fact. The proud young French king said, you remember, when someone spoke of the State, "I am the State," but, not with arrogance, not with egotism, in simplicity and truth, Jesus said: "I am the way, the truth and the life." Jesus is the gospel. The gospel is not a creed simply, is not a society of priests, the gospel comes to us embodied in a person. Jesus is himself the gospel; receiving him we receive the power of God unto salvation. Have we a right to think lightly of Jesus who is the most important personage of the world's history, who is the center of the Scriptures?

And thirdly, Jesus is a being unique in the universe. God the pure spirit, is only God, and man, strange being that he is, is only man; but Jesus—the Scriptures require us to believe it—Jesus is both, truly God and truly man. I do not wonder that persons shrink away from that fact, it is stupendous, it is inconceivable in one sense, yet it is the plain teaching of God's Word. He is not simply a man, he has risen

from us to divinity. He is not simply God taking upon him some outward semblance of humanity. He is truly God and truly man—truly
each. His divinity: why friends, it lies plain on the surface of God's
Word. Plain people, unsophisticated, who just read it right along and
take it as it is, cannot well help seeing that. I pray you remember,
God's word was not written for learned divines, for skillful com-
mentators, for skeptical inquirers, God's word was written for the people. It is a handbook for practical guidance.

Therefore, whatever lies plain on the surface of God's Word, not
in one phrase alone but in many places, that is exceedingly apt to be
what is meant. Bible learning is all a good thing in its place, but after
all if we want to get practical truth for our own guidance out of God's
Word we shall be most likely to get its meaning more clearly and truly
if we take the plain meaning of the passage that lies on the surface to
any unsophisticated observer. You might as well pluck the throbbing
heart out of this bosom and call what is left a living man as to take
the divinity of Jesus Christ out of this book and call the rest God's
Word. It is set forth in a thousand ways in all parts of the Scriptures
and if anyone should ask me to mention three or four passages why
here they are: "In the beginning was the Word and the Word was
with God and the Word was God. And the Word was made flesh and
dwelt among us—full of grace and truth." And when Thomas after his
long doubting was convinced, he cried, "My Lord and my God." If he
to whom he said it had been a mere man, he would have shrunk
from such an idolatrous utterance, but he commended him for saying
it.

On the other hand the Scriptures as plainly set forth Jesus as having
a human nature. The Christian world has long been half oblivious of
the humanity of Christ. It is only until now that men are beginning to
realize the humanity of him who is also divine—the carpenter of
Nazareth who worked with hard hands over homely toil. A great many
of those who try to lead the masses offer speculative delusions and
talk against Christ and Christianity. Why don't they tell the people
that the founder of Christianity was in the truest sense a working man
and the friend of the poor? His humanity made it possible that he
should be really tempted. Why could not any human nature be
tempted? Our first parents in their Eden, in their purity, were tempted
and fell. The high angels were tempted and fell out of heaven. The
humanity of Christ could not morally be overcome with sin due to the
influence of the Holy Ghost, yet the humanity of Christ could be
tempted, and the temptation could be a reality. As man he could take
our place before God, he could suffer in our stead, he could die and

rise again for us, and his divinity gave to that suffering, atoning death and resurrection a dignity and significance.

My friends, these souls of ours crave a perfect example. We need imperfect examples such as the Scriptures furnish and life furnishes us every day, of every grade and condition, but then our souls crave an ideal of perfection, and there it is, a perfect example, at the summit of them all—a perfect example in the humanity of our Lord and Saviour. As man he gives assurance of his sympathy with his having been tempted only once like as we are, yet without sin. Oh, how wonderful is the fact! I often pause to dwell on it, that not only do tempted ones in this life bow safe around the glorious throne, but one who was tempted here sits upon the throne, and we know that he can sympathize with our infirmities, with our temptations, with our trials, and being unique, in all, exists the God-man. When he stood upon the Mount of Olives do you not remember how he said: "All authority and power in heaven and earth is given unto me," and "Lo, I am with you alway, even unto the end of the world"? Who over all the nations, who over all ages, has a right to think lightly of Jesus?

In the fourth place, Jesus has wrought a work that is unparalleled in its nature and in its importance. It is the most wonderful that has ever occurred in the universe. It is not creation, it is redemption. It is reconciliation between the holy ruler of the universe and the beings who have broken his law. A work so wonderful it is that the Scriptures give us an intimation that the most exalted creatures of God that do exist, look down amid all the world's wonders and wonder most at this. Nay, with the strange perversity which we human beings show about many things, there are many persons who cannot believe it because it is so wonderful. It seems impossible that the maker and ruler of the universe should have chosen such a stage to do these things. The theater is too small; the stage is too insignificant for such a drama as the atonement, they say. Well, nearly all the most important things in this world have had comparatively an unimportant theater. Daniel Webster had evidently thought of this when he wrote these words to be placed on his tombstone: "Philosophical argument, especially that drawn from the vestures of the material universe, and the apparent insignificance of our world have sometimes shaken my reason for the faith that is in me, but my heart has always assured and reassured me that the mission of Jesus Christ is a divine reality."

There is no need to have our faith shaken when we remember what I have said; the most insignificant spot of earth may be the scene of earth's greatest events. And this little earth came to be, as the Scriptures declare, the scene of the mightiest event of the universe, the reconciliation of God's creatures to himself.

Now once more, Jesus sustains, and must sustain, a personal relation to each one of us. I do not mean as a matter of history—there is a sense of course in which every person has a relation to each of us—but I mean as the loving Saviour. He must by the very necessity of things sustain a personal relation to each of us. We can as well shake off our own being as to prevent the necessity of that personal relation to him. We can determine its character, we can be his friends, by the grace of God, otherwise we are, we cannot but be his enemies. There are those who think they can live neutral with reference to Christianity, who think they can treat Christian mysteries, and people in general, with a certain respect, and be kind and courteous, and play neutral. But O my friends, it is not my saying, merely Jesus himself has said "he that is not with me is against me." "He that gathereth not with me, scattereth." There is no neutrality. We must be his friends or we are his foes, delude ourselves as we may.

The most important question of life is, "What is a man's relationship to Jesus?" And that turns upon another question, "What does a man think and feel about himself?" Jesus came not to call righteous men, but sinners to repentance. If I am a sinner, if I have been trying hard to do right, and have learned more and more how hard it is for me to do right, if my own conscience condemns, therefore God who is greater than my heart must condemn me. If I am troubled how my guilt shall be removed, and my sinfulness, then Jesus is for me, and then I am for Jesus. But if I feel that I am a good kind of person, fond of comparing myself with my fellow men, looking upon my faults as reasonable defects, then no wonder I get so fanciful theories about Jesus. Then I am not in the position from which he came to relieve me.

O my friends, what is your relation to Jesus? It is the question of all questions: what is your relation to Jesus? It is a question which you should settle in your honest heart, and the decision you reach you ought to proclaim to your fellow men: for he said: "Whosoever shall confess, I will myself confess, and whosoever shall deny me"—and to refuse to confess him is to deny him—"him will I also deny before the angels which are in heaven." O my friends, what is your personal relation to Jesus? It is a question which you can postpone now, if you will, but it will come back again and again. It is a question which will face you. You will face it in the day for which all other days were made; in the day when before the Saviour, you shall stand, and he your judge. In that day every knee shall bow, and shall confess, willing or unwilling, that Jesus is Christ his Lord, to God the Father. O my friends, prepare for that day by turning to Christ now! What is your personal relationship to Jesus? Confess him now!

6

COME UNTO ME

Come unto me, all ye that labor and are heavy laden, and I will give you rest. Take my yoke upon you, and learn of me; for I am meek and lowly in heart: and ye shall find rest unto your souls. For my yoke is easy, and my burden is light. MATTHEW 11:28–30

THIS familiar passage of Scripture contains one of the most precious among the many precious invitations of our compassionate Redeemer. Many a feeble and fainting believer has been led by it to take fresh courage and "press toward the mark," many a burdened sinner has found in it that the gospel of Jesus is indeed "good news," "a word in season to him that is weary." And since the passage is so important and so precious, we may find our profit in attending a little to its phraseology, in endeavoring to make ourselves acquainted with its precise terms.

The Saviour invites to him all "that labor and are heavy laden." In this he doubtless referred partly to the burden of ceremonies and observances which the scribes and Pharisees imposed upon their followers, as required by the traditions of the fathers, and as essential and sufficient for their finding favor with God. The law itself, St. Paul tells us, was, if looked upon as a means of salvation, too grievous a burden for any to bear; and these superstitious observances made it yet more grievous. Such persons, then, toiling and borne down beneath the burden of the ceremonial law, are here invited to the Saviour. But he had reference likewise to all men, Jew and Gentile, in every nation and age, who are burdened with *sin*. All such are invited to him, with the promise that he will give them rest, rest from their labor, and relief from their load. They wear the galling yoke of sin and Satan, and he bids them take *his* yoke upon them.

Wearing the yoke of another is an expression very often employed in Scripture (as all will remember) to denote *subjection* to him. The figure is taken, of course, from beasts of burden, as oxen; being ap-

plied thence to all who are the laboring servants of a master. Jesus is
then bidding those who have been the "servants of sin," to obey him
from the heart and be *his* servants; those who have been subject to
Satan, to take *him* instead as their King. "Take my yoke upon you,
and learn of me." He recommends himself not only as King and Master, but as Teacher too. The gospel is frequently and properly represented as something to be *learned;* men need to be *taught* the way of
salvation. Thus we read that God "will have all men to be saved, and
to come to a knowledge of the truth." This knowledge of the truth,
these lessons of salvation, must be obtained from the Great Teacher
Jesus.

And when he says, "For I am meek and lowly in heart," the Saviour
means to show that he is fitted to be a Teacher, that so all may come
and learn of him. In order that a Teacher may win the hearts of his
pupils, and thereby the better make them love to learn and love what
they do learn, he must unite to other qualities a certain mildness, and
gentleness, and kindliness. Such men, other things being equal, are
always most beloved and most successful. There are some men who
by their affection and gentleness seem able to win at once the love
of a child. And when our blessed Saviour bids men learn of him,
he encourages the timid and fearful to come to him, by telling them
that he is meek and lowly in heart, mild and loving and gentle, that
he will be kind to them, and they need not fear. He would not be
rough and overbearing and haughty as were the Doctors, the teachers
of the law, he is not imperious and domineering and severe like many
who have since professed to teach his doctrines: he is humble and affectionate, condescending and kind.

We may learn from these words the character of the lessons, as well
as of the Teacher. It is the knowledge of himself that he will give; and
as he is meek and lowly, i.e., gentle and humble, so those that come
to learn of him will be taught lessons of gentleness, lessons of humility.
Still the chief intent of this clause would seem to be what was mentioned first, namely to recommend himself as disposed to be kind and
affectionate to all who might come to learn of him. "Take my yoke
upon you, and learn of me: [you need not fear to make me your
Teacher, for I am meek and lowly in heart:] and ye shall find rest
unto your souls." He promises to free them from their grievous toils,
to relieve them of their heavy burdens, to give them *rest*. To appreciate fully the expressiveness of this figure, one must imagine himself
bearing a heavy burden, a weight such as he can hardly sustain, and
that after bearing it till he is almost crushed to the ground, he throws
it off, and rests. There are few things so delightful as this *rest* to one

who has been heavy laden. And then suppose the burden is clinging to you, bound with cords you cannot sever, though you are bowed down under the load and vainly striving to throw it off, and that as you labor thus and are heavy laden, one offers if you come to him to loose the bonds and take away the burden, and let you rest—how sweet would be the thought! how quickly, how joyfully, how thankfully, you would run to him!

But it is impossible that men should be without subjection to some higher power; by our very nature we look up to some Being that is above us. All who are not subject to God, are the subjects of Satan: and they who wish to be delivered from the dominion of the Evil One, must find such deliverance in having God himself for their King, as he intended they should when he made them. Accordingly, when the Saviour offers to give rest, he bids them take *his* yoke upon them, and learn of *him,* and they shall find rest unto their souls. And then he concludes the invitation by encouraging them to believe that this exchange will be good and pleasant; they *labor* under the galling yoke of Satan, and are *heavy laden* with the grievous burdens of sin, but *his* yoke is *easy.* This burden is *light.* Such, I think, is the meaning of the various passages of this invitation, which, familiar as it is, I may read again: "Come unto me, all ye that labor and are heavy laden, and I will give you rest. Take my yoke upon you, and learn of me; for I am meek and lowly in heart: and ye shall find rest unto your souls. For my yoke is easy, and my burden is light." (Matt. 11:28–30).

Having endeavored thus to explain the language of the text, I wish to say something upon two subjects connected with it, (1) who they are that are here invited to come and (2) what is meant by *coming* to Jesus.

I. The invitations of the gospel are addressed to all; the gospel is to be preached to every creature. God commandeth all men everywhere to repent, he promises that whosoever believeth on Jesus shall not perish, but have everlasting life, and "whosoever will," is invited to take of the water of life, freely. The purposes of Him who inhabiteth eternity, and who seeth the end from the beginning, will all be fulfilled. Those purposes we cannot declare, that God will have (i.e., wishes) all men to be saved, that he bids all the ends of the earth look unto him, that he that cometh unto Jesus shall in no wise be cast out.

And it is worth observing that the gospel invitations, while they extend to all, are so varied. The same bountiful and gracious Being who suits the blessings of his providence to our various wants, does also adapt the invitations of his mercy to the varied characters and conditions of men. Are men enemies to God?—they are invited to be reconciled. Have they hearts harder than the nether millstone?—he offers to take away the stone, and give a heart of flesh. Are they dancing gaily, or rushing madly, along the way that leads to death?—he calls upon them to turn, "Turn ye, turn ye, for why will ye die?" Are they sleeping the heavy sleep of sin?—"Awake thou that sleepest, and arise from the dead." Are men hungering with a craving hunger? —he tells them of the bread that came down from heaven. Are they thirsty?—he calls them to the water of life. And are they burdened with sin and sinfulness?—he invites them to come to Jesus for rest. It is those who are "bowed down beneath a load of sin," that are here especially invited to come to Jesus.

Sin is great and grievous burden: and no man can ever see it as it is and feel it in its weight without wishing to be relieved of it. My hearers, are there not many among you who have often felt this—who have often felt heavy laden with the load of your transgressions, and the burden of your sinfulness? Are there not those among you who feel this now? If you do not all feel so, it is because your perceptions are blunted, you do not see things as they are. You have been servants of sin for a long time—have you not found it a hard master? You have been wearing the yoke of Satan lo! these many years—have you not found that his yoke is indeed galling and grievous? How many things you have done at his bidding that you knew to be wrong? How often you have stifled the voice of your conscience, and listened to the suggestions of the Tempter! How often you have toiled to gratify sinful desires and passions, and found that still the craving, aching void was left unfilled!

What has sin done for the world and for you that you should desire it? It brought death into the world, and all our woe. It has filled the earth with suffering and sorrow. It has made it needful that Jesus, the only-begotten Son of God, should suffer and die, to make atonement for it. It has brought upon *you* much of unhappiness now, and many most fearful apprehensions for the future. By your sins you have incurred the just anger of Him that made you—already they rise mountain high, and yet still you go on in your sinfulness, accumulating more and more, *heaping* up wrath against the day of wrath. You shudder when you think of death, you tremble when you think of God, for you know well that you are not prepared to die, that you cannot meet your Maker and Judge in peace. And not only has sin brought on you all these sufferings and fears, but you cannot rid yourself of it. You have bowed your neck to the yoke, and now you cannot free yourself from it. Never did any old man of the sea cling so closely upon the shoulders of the deluded traveler, as the hideous form of sin clings to you, and you cannot shake it off, struggle as you may. No poisoned garment of ancient fable ever adhered so closely to him that wore it, sending death through all his frame, as does the garment of iniquity.

Sum it up again—what has sin done for you? It has made you unhappy, filling you with craving, unsatisfied desires, it has made you captive, and bound you with cords you cannot burst, it has brought upon you the indignation and wrath of Almighty God, which you cannot expiate. Is it not then a burden, of which you would like to be relieved? If so, hear the Saviour's own invitation, and come to him. He will take off the heavy load that crushes you, and you shall find rest to your souls. He will intercede in your behalf before God, he will take away your guilt by the sacrifice he has offered, he will "wash you thoroughly from your iniquity, and cleanse you from your sin."

Let all then, who are burdened with sin and sinfulness, who long to know how their transgressions may be forgiven and their souls saved, all who are inquiring what they must do, let them hear the gracious words of the text, and come to Jesus.

Do you fear that God is angry with you, and will not hear your prayer? It is true. God is angry with the wicked every day; and the sacrifice of the wicked is an abomination unto the Lord. You may not mock the offended majesty of God Most High, you may not dare to mock him by coming unto him in your own name, and trusting in your own righteousness. You ought to fear before him, and to tremble at the thought of coming to him thus. But you may come to Jesus— you are invited to come to him. He is the appointed mediator between God and man. Come and ask him to intercede for you. And then through him draw near to the throne of grace. Make mention of his merits, plead his atoning sacrifice, rely wholly on what he has done, and God's anger is turned away—he will hear, he will pardon, and your soul shall live. If then you are burdened with a sense of your unworthiness, come to Jesus, and you shall not come in vain.

All that labor, with whatever toil, all that are heavy laden, with whatever burden, may take this invitation as addressed to them. "Thou callest burdened souls to Thee, And such, O Lord, am I." Whatever it is that bears you down, the consciousness of sin, the terror of judgment, distressing doubts or manifold temptations, whatever else may torment your soul and weigh down your spirit, this invitation is for you. If you are burdened with affliction or sorrow or fearful apprehension, in short (to repeat it again and again) if you bear any burden, you are invited to Jesus. "Come unto me, *all* ye," etc.

It would be natural and reasonable enough for one thus frequently and earnestly invited to come to Jesus, especially for one who is "an alien from God, and a stranger to grace," who knows not the blessed Saviour in the pardon of his sins, who has never "come boldly unto the throne of grace," and obtained mercy and found grace to help in time of need, it would be natural enough for him to inquire now, "What is *meant* by coming to Jesus? Suppose I feel myself to be burdened, and want to seek relief, how shall I come to Jesus for rest?" This is the remaining subject of which I propose to speak. I shall not try to explain, for I can add nothing to that which is, in itself, plain already, but only to illustrate.

First then I say, come to him as men came when he was on earth. We sometimes hear it said, "Oh, that I had lived when Jesus was sojourning among men; how would I have gone to him for peace and prayed that I might follow him whithersoever he went! What a privilege it must have been to the people of Bethany, for instance, when again and again Jesus came among them, when they might, even in their own homes, sit as Mary sat at the feet of the great and good Teacher and learn lessons of heavenly wisdom!" Yes, it was a great privilege; and it is true that the case is somewhat different now. We cannot now go sensibly to Jesus as a man, living somewhere among us. We are not now to go from one part of the country or the world to another, in order to be where the Saviour is. There is no sensible coming to him now. But it is only a change from *sight* to *faith*—from a moving of the body to a moving of the thoughts and affections. It may be thought a great privation that we cannot go somewhere, as they did then, and find him. But is it not on the other hand a great privilege that we need not now go anywhere, we may always find him here? He is everywhere, and as much in one place as another. Men have often forgotten this great and consoling and gladdening truth. Many a weary pilgrimage has been made in the centuries that are past to the Holy Land, in the hope that forgiveness of sin and peace of conscience, which could not be found at home, might be found there. It is pleasant, and may do the heart good, to stand where Jesus stood, to weep where he wept on Olivet, to pray where he prayed in Gethsemane, but he is here now as well as there. Wherever one seeks him there he may be found "For where two or three are gathered together in my name, there am I in the midst of them." Wherever there is a tear of penitence, or a sigh of godly sorrow, wherever there is earnest prayer to him or the desire to pray felt in the heart, there is Jesus to see and to hear and to answer.

If then we lose the sensible coming, do we not gain greatly in that we can always find him where we are? And since this is so, since he is really and always near to every one that seeketh him, may I not say again, come to him as men came when he was on earth. Come with the same confidence in his power that they felt who asked him to heal their disease. There are many to testify that they have come and been heard, and none been sent empty away—do you come, and you too shall hear him say, "Thy sins are forgiven thee." Come with the same humility the Syrophoenician woman felt, when she pled that the dogs, though they should not eat the children's food, might yet have the crumbs that fell under the table—and that she, though a Gentile, might yet have some humble share in that salvation which was of the Jews. Come with all the earnestness the poor blind man felt. He heard that Jesus was passing, and none could hinder him with all their charges, from crying, "Jesus, thou son of David, have mercy on me." And when the compassionate Saviour stopped, and commanded him to be called, they said to him, "Be of good comfort, rise! he calleth thee." Even so, my hearer, Jesus commands you to be called, as you sit in your spiritual blindness. Just as Bartimeus threw away his cloak that nothing might hinder him, and went eagerly to Jesus, so you come at once unto him, and ask that you may receive your sight. You too shall hear him say, "Go thy way; thy faith hath made thee whole."

Again, and this is the last thing I shall say now, come to Jesus just as you are. Wait not to be ready—think not of being prepared—dream not of being fit, to come. The readiness, the preparation, the fitness, all must be his gift. How wrong to put off your coming to him till you have that which he alone can give. You are a burdened sinner—is it not so? Do you not feel the truth, here on my heart the burden lies, past offenses pain mine eyes—you are heavy laden with sin—then Jesus here invites you to come unto him. Do you say you are not sorry for sin as you ought to be? I know you are not. But come to Jesus, and ask that he will help you to repent. If you have no faith, ask that he will give you faith. All must come from him. Let him be your Lord, your life, your sacrifice, your Saviour and your all. You are a sinner, and Jesus Christ came into the world to save sinners.

It is said (many here have doubtless read the account) that a brother of the famous Whitefield was once conversing, in great distress, with Lady Huntingdon. She told him of the infinite love and mercy of Jesus, but he replied, "I know all that; but there is no mercy for me—I am *lost,* I am *lost.*" "I am glad to hear it, Mr. Whitefield, very glad to hear it." "How, my dear Madam, glad to hear that I am lost?" "Yes, Jesus came to save the lost." That word moved him;

he believed on Jesus, and lived and died a Christian. And so may you, if you believe on him who is the Saviour of the lost and ruined. Then come to Jesus, come earnestly, come just as you are.

> Just as I am, without one plea
> Save that thy blood was shed for me,
> And that thou bidst me come to thee,
> O Lamb of God, I come.

Come, and you will be heard—you shall find rest. He will not send you away. He came into the world to save sinners—he suffered and died to save sinners—he invited burdened sinners to him. Then take this blessed, this precious invitation to yourself, come to Jesus, and your soul shall live. "And the Spirit and the bride say, Come. And let him that heareth say, Come. And let him that is athirst come. And whosoever will, let him take the water of life freely."

7

THE LORD'S PRAYER

Our Father which art in heaven, Hallowed be thy name.
MATTHEW 6:9

THE prayer which thus begins, which for many ages has been called
among Christians "the Lord's Prayer," is above all eulogium for its
sweetness. No wonder this is so! For our Lord presents it as a specimen, as a model of prayer. He said, "When ye pray, use not vain repetitions, as the heathen do: for they think that they shall be heard for
their much speaking," saying over the same thing a thousand times.
"Be ye not therefore like unto them: for your Father knoweth what
things ye have need of, before ye ask him." *Thus* then do *ye* pray—
this way and not with vain repetitions, not with much speaking, *thus*
do ye pray! He gives it as a sample, as a model. So on a later occasion,
recorded in the 11th Chapter of Luke—probably a long time after
this, most likely in quite another part of the country, certainly on a
later occasion—our Lord was praying himself, and when he ceased,
the disciples asked him "Teach us to pray" and he said "When ye
pray, say:" and then he gave them substantially the same prayer
as the one here before us.

Now it very naturally occurs to many persons that our Lord has
given this as a *form* of prayer; that when we pray we ought always
to say these words. I do not object to using these words whenever
anyone thinks them appropriate, that they express his sentiments; but
it is very certain that our Lord did not give this as a form of prayer.
If you will notice a moment I shall prove it. On the second occasion
the prayer is very different from that which we here read. Even in the
common text, it is different in several expressions; but if you will
take any revised text as furnished by any competent scholar of the
day, you will find that the prayer on that occasion is quite different.
Allow me to repeat it as it is there. You all know the words as they
occur here but on that second occasion this is what he said: "Father,
Hallowed be thy name. Thy kingdom come. Give us day by day our
daily bread. And forgive us our sins; for we also forgive every one

66

that is indebted to us. And bring us not into temptation."

Now you observe that I have omitted several phrases of the familiar prayer given here in the Sermon on the Mount. If you look a little closely you notice that nothing of essential importance, no distinctive idea, has been omitted here. Instead of "Our Father which art in heaven," you have simply "Father." You have lost some pleasing words, but you have really lost no part of the essential thought. When after the petition "Thy kingdom come," you find wanting the words "Thy will be done on earth as it is in heaven," you observe in a moment that although a pleasing expression has been expunged, it is involved in the preceding petition, "Thy kingdom come;" for when God's reign on earth is fully come, his will must of necessity be done on earth as in heaven. And so, when after the prayer "Bring us not into temptation," you miss the words "But deliver us from evil," you observe that they do, at most, but express the other side of the same truth; something that is implied in the words that remain.

On that second occasion then, our Lord has omitted no idea that belongs to the prayer. It is substantially the very same, but in form it is exceedingly different. Is not there the proof at once that he did not intend this as a form of prayer? If he did so intend, why in the world should he not have repeated his form correctly on the second occasion? No: he intended it not as a form of prayer, that precisely these words should be used, but as an example, "Thus do ye pray." Avoid the vain repetitions and much speaking of the heathen: Thus: thus comprehensively; thus simply. Oh, how much is included in these few, brief, simply expressed petitions! "Thus then do ye pray."

And my brethren, I venture to ask your special attention to this model in one respect. We have two good classes of petitions here, as is obvious at once, petitions with reference to God's glory, and petitions with reference to our own good. And my point is, that the petitions with reference to God's glory come first. Now you have noticed, and indeed it seems natural to us that when we pray, we pray first about ourselves, and a great deal about ourselves, and then if we do not forget, if there seems to be time left before we close the prayer, we may introduce some petitions as to God's glory. But here the class of petitions which refer to God's glory come first. That is their rightful place. I do not feel they should always come first in order, that there ought to be any formality or stiffness in it, but that they should often be put in the place of priority, and regularly in the place of pre-eminence. Much more important is it that God's name should be hallowed, and God's kingdom come in the world, than that you and I, as individuals, should gain the blessings we desire.

And now I propose to you, that while of course we cannot bring out many of the thoughts involved in this comprehensive prayer, we shall try to get some practical lessons from it.

I. Observe first, the petitions which relate to God's glory.

1. "Hallowed be thy name." The words are so simple, we have known them so well from our childhood, that it is really difficult to stop and ask what they mean. Let thy name be made holy. God's name represents himself. It is a prayer that his name, and himself as represented by his name, may be regarded as holy—spoken of as holy—treated as holy. We have a model here in the picture given by Isaiah, the adoring Seraphs covering their faces in awe before the throne. What do they cry? Not, as often we do; great, majestic, glorious—not a word about his power, nor even about his wisdom—"Holy, Holy, Holy, Lord God of Hosts." That is the central thought, that ought to be our deepest desire, that God may be regarded, and spoken of, and treated, as *holy*.

Oh, what a contrast between that scene of the vision, and the sights and the souls of this world in which we live. Walk the streets anywhere; listen to the talk wherever you find it, especially when men grow excited. Hear them! Hear how that high and holy name is bandied as a jest and polluted with profanity. It is enough to make a man shiver to hear the profanity that abounds everywhere. I have shivered, literally, sometimes as I listened.

But my brethren, have we nothing to do but to look with horror at other men's profanity? There are some things important to our own life here. Have a care that while you may not use in vain the sacred name of God itself, you shall not fall into the practice of using other sacred expressions lightly and irreverently. I have heard even refined ladies use phrases in a light way, that were appropriate only in solemn prayer; and to a certain extent that was irreverence, that was profanity. Have a care about indulging wit that comes from profaning the language of Scripture, and allusions to God. Bluff old Dr. Johnson once said that "a man that has any respect for himself ought to be above that kind of wit, it is so cheap: any one can do that." Yes, anyone that has any respect for himself ought to be above that kind of wit, and a man that has any reverence for God ought to shrink from it. Have a care how you repeat the profanity of other men. You want to tell a good story and the point of it perhaps lies in a profane expression. Now is it that you should repeat that expression? Is it good for yourself to repeat it? Is it healthy? Especially is it good for that boy there that is hearing, and may not make the nice distinction that you make, when you repeat other men's profanity? I would not inculcate scrupulosity about trifles, but perchance this is not a trifle, and it seems to me that we who pray this prayer, ought to lay such things to our hearts, and shrink with horror, and cultivate ourselves into shrinking with shuddering, from anything like profanity. Oh, that God's name might always be spoken with deepest reverence. Oh, that God himself might come to be everywhere thought of, and talked about, and obeyed, as holy. Anyhow, let us try to have it so in our hearts, on our lips, in our lives.

2. And the second petition, "Thy reign come." I am not going to explain all these simple words of course, but here is one that wants explaining. The Greek word which is rendered "kingdom" in the text requires three English words to convey its meaning. Primarily the word means "kingship," the condition of being a king, the possession of royal power. Then secondarily it means "reign," the exercise of royal power. As a final derivation it means what we call "kingdom," subjects or territory over whom or in which this royal power is exercised. Kingship, and reign, and kingdom. There are many cases of that kind in translation, where several terms have to be used in one language to convey the meaning of a single word in another. Now the leading thought here is evidently that which we express by the word "reign." And the reference is to the Messianic reign which the prophets had long foretold; that Messianic reign of which David had sung; that Messianic reign which John the Baptist had declared was now near at hand, and Jesus at the beginning of his ministry in Galilee took up the same cry, "The kingdom of heaven is near at hand; repent therefore and believe the good tidings." Men had long prayed that that reign might come, and now there was all the more propriety in such a prayer, for it was near at hand.

Do you think there is no need of that prayer still? Do you think the reign, the Messianic reign of God in the world, has come? It has but begun. It was beginning when Jesus taught these teachings. It began still more when he rose triumphant from the grave and ascended glorious into the sky. It began still further, on the day of Pentecost. It began in another sense at the destruction of Jerusalem, which he spoke of beforehand as the time when he should come in his kingdom. It has begun on the earth, ah! it has not come yet. Alas, for the wide portions of the world where the very name of the King Messiah has not come. Alas, in the metropolis of one of the great Christian nations of today, the great mass of the men that surge around us, are utterly unsanctified by the gospel, utterly heedless of the reign of God. Stop any moment and think, between two heartbeats, of this great world you live in, of this great city you live in, and then you shall address yourself with new fervor to the prayer: "Thy reign come,

O God! thy reign!" Anyhow, let it come in us; let it pervade our whole being; let it control our whole life; let it sanctify our home life; let it elevate our social life; let it purify our business life; let men feel, as they note our conduct, that we are subjects of the Lord God.

3. I shall not dwell, for lack of time, upon the third petition here, which is but an expansion of the preceding. For, as I have said, whenever God's reign has fully come, then his will must be done on earth. Many things occur now that are not according to God's will. The prayer is that God's will may take place; that everything may happen on earth in accordance with God's will, as in heaven everything does happen. Many times for us, I know it is hard even to *consent* that this shall be so. When it is plainly God's will that something should happen, which to us is painful, we shrink and with difficulty we say, "Thy will be done." No wonder: it has been so with better persons than we are. Certain disciples, when they besought Paul not to go up to Jerusalem and he would not be persuaded, ceased and said: "The will of the Lord be done." The struggling Saviour in Gethsemane as he strove in agony and prayer to nerve himself up for what he had to bear, said again and again—for it would not stay said: "nevertheless, not my will, but thine be done." No wonder we find it hard sometimes to say that. The prayer teaches us not merely to submit to God's will, but to desire that God's will may take place in the world; that everything concerning us and concerning all around us may happen according to his will. And if he takes away our property, our health, our usefulness, our life, or some one we love better than our life, still we would say and we should rejoice when we say, "Thy will be done." Oh, if it could be so; if in the world, whether gaining or losing, in success or failure, it could be so, in us and about us, that God's will were done in all things—what a joy in the thought; what a springing gladness it puts into the heart, the very idea!

II. But perhaps we shall find, not more important but more practical lessons if we turn to the second part of the prayer, which contains petitions relating to ourselves.

1. First: "Give us this day our daily bread." Now I entreat you, don't listen to the commentaries, so many of which tell you that this means spiritual bread. I am weary of that everlasting spiritualizing. Spiritual things are far above temporal things, but there are many references in the Scriptures to our temporal and material wants, and why should we lose their meaning, and sustaining power, because we go on allegorizing everything. It is plainly a prayer for temporal good, as represented by that which is most essential, and thus stated in the simplest possible form; and a prayer with reference simply to day

after day. A little child sees its meaning and feels its sweetness, and the wisest man can find no higher wisdom than to cry still: "Give us this day our daily bread."

My brethren, I should be inclined to think that above all the petitions of the prayer this needs to be enforced in our time. I have known some Christians who were very unwilling to realize that there was any human exertion in obtaining spiritual good. They say, if that be true, how is it the gift of God? And if it be the gift of God, how can it be the effort of our own labor? Yet if spiritual good is the gift of God, so is temporal good the gift of God, though it is obtained only by human effort. The truth is, we see, that both are the gift of God, and both are the result of our own exertions.

Especially with reference to one of the great tendencies of thought in our time is it important that we should cherish this petition for our daily bread. "Pshaw!" men say, "that depends upon physical forces and laws; upon material things; upon your own exertion, man; upon the climate and the weather." Now in the face of these notions it becomes all the more appropriate that we should pray to God to give us daily bread. Yes, and I tell you plainly and boldly, though I have not time to develop the thought, if it is not right and wise to ask God for daily bread, if as they tell you in the newspapers so often, there is no efficacy in prayer, there is no use in praying for rain, then there is no God at all. You are driven straight to it by absolute logical necessity. If it is not proper to pray for daily bread and to pray for rain, there is no God; there is nothing in existence but matter, with its organization and its results. You cannot help it, there is no standing room, for the life of you, between those two positions. Alas, alas, how many in our time, one-sided or superficial, have gone into utter materialism. Never was there a time when it was more needful that the Christian world should realize in their experience the sentiment of this prayer. We work for daily bread, and we plan for years to come, but none the less are we to seek it as the daily gift of the daily goodness of our Father in heaven.

2. "And forgive us our debts, as we forgive our debtors." The simple prayer for temporal things all embraced in that one petition for what is most indispensable, and now in addition, a twofold prayer—forgiveness for past sin, and deliverance from sin in the future. That our God may be glorified; that our earthly wants may be supplied, and that we may be forgiven our sin, and delivered from evil—that is all there is to pray for.

You know that the term "debt" is used here as an Aramaic expression to denote sin—sin regarded as a debt, which we must pay to God, or in the kindred phrase of other languages, "pay the penalty." You notice that when our Lord repeats the thought a moment later he say trespasses, or transgressions. You remember that when he gives the prayer on a subsequent occasion it is: "Forgive us our sins; for we also forgive everyone that is indebted to us." "Forgive us our debts" means, forgive us our sins. My friends, does it ever occur to you that you are more anxious about the "give" than the "forgive"? Does it ever happen in your experience that you pray that God would give and forget to ask that God would forgive? And yet, is not this last as deep a need? Yea, a deeper need than the other? Ah! that a man should have all earthly things given him, and his sins not forgiven, would be a poor gift. Yet a man who should be deprived of all earthly things and go starving into the other world, yet with his sins forgiven, would be rich and might rejoice. Let us not forget as we go on praying for what God has to give, to ask still more earnestly that he would forgive us our sins.

I must beg you in connection with the prayer to dwell upon the condition which our Lord here presents. It is a matter of the utmost practical importance to all of us. "Forgive us our debts, as we forgive our debtors." You have noticed surely, that after completing this simple prayer, Jesus before going on to speak of other things, takes up again one of the thoughts of the prayer; and which one is it? Something about God's name being hallowed, or his reign coming? Something about daily bread? Something about temptation, or evil? Nay: it is this one; this one thought he repeats, repeats it positively and negatively. For if you forgive men their trespasses, your Heavenly Father will also forgive you, and if you forgive not, neither will your Heavenly Father forgive you. You know why—you know yourself but little if you do not well know why he dwells upon this. The disposition to be revengeful, or at any rate to be unforgiving, is one of the deepest rooted, one of the hardest to correct, one of the most hurtful and ruinous in its influence, of all the evil dispositions that belong to our sinful human nature. So our Lord presents forgiving as the condition of being forgiven, the condition *sine qua non*—if we do not forgive men we cannot be forgiven. He does not mean that our forgiving in the meritorious ground of our being forgiven. It is an indispensable condition. Only if we do forgive men can we be forgiven, but then we are forgiven on the ground which the gospel provides— the merit which is not our own.

Now let us make a practical distinction. We use that word "forgive" in a somewhat ambiguous fashion. In the strict and proper sense it is not our duty to forgive a man unless he repents. God forgives in that sense no man but the penitent, and Jesus said, you remember: "If thy brother sin against thee seven times in the day and seven times in the day turn saying, 'I repent,' thou shalt forgive him." It is not right that you should restore a man to the confidence he has forfeited, unless he shows himself worthy of it. It is not right that you should forgive a man, in the full sense of the term, unless he repents; not only is it not your duty, but it is not right. "Love your enemies, that ye may be sons of your Father in heaven." God forgives only the penitent, and loves them as his friends, but even the impenitent God loves. "He makes his sun to rise on the evil and the good, and sends rain on the just and the unjust." He wishes his enemies no harm, but does them good. We need not, and really should not, forgive a man in the full sense while he remains impenitent, but we must in the other sense forgive him. We must bear him no malice. We must do him no harm. We must be glad to do him good, in anything that will not promote his evil designs against us. Thus shall we be the sons of our Father in heaven.

I think this distinction is practically important. The idea of forgiving a man who is impenitent does seem to be impracticable, and that is not what the Scriptures teach; but that we should bear no malice and yield to no revenge, that is what the Scriptures teach. Ah me, even this is hard enough for poor human nature! Let us strive to do that; let us lay it to heart. Who is there here today among us who has not sometimes thought himself to have been cruelly wronged? Who? We all have need then to exercise this forgiveness.

3. And finally, "bring us not into temptation." For it is not simply *lead,* it is *bring.* Human agency is, for the moment, here left out of account. The thought is, of God's providence as bearing us on, and bringing us into certain situations, and the prayer is that God will not bring us into circumstances of temptation of trial. Why? Because we are afraid we cannot stand temptation. Ah, every man that knows himself will most certainly feel an echo in his heart, "I am weak, O Lord, bring me not into temptation."

A man advertised for a coachman, and when the applicants came, he asked each one, "How near would you undertake to run my carriage wheel to the edge of a precipice?" The first one said he would run within a foot of it. The second said he would run within six inches. The third was an Irishman, who said, "I would kape away as far as I could,"—and he got the place. Maybe you will remember that, if you forget my solemn injunction. O my Christian friends, pray that you may be kept away from temptation, for you are weak, and let him that thinketh he standeth, take heed lest he fall.

"Bring us not into temptation, but deliver us from evil."

My brethren, this simple prayer ought as a model to control all our praying. Its spirit ought to strike into our blood, shaping our whole character, regulating our whole life. And as we pray it, oh, ought not our life's endeavor to accord with it? What folly to pray, "Thy reign come," and never a finger lifted to urge forward the progress of that reign; never a sacrifice made, never deed done, nor word spoken, nought but idle prayer. What folly to pray for forgiveness of sin, and pray for deliverance from evil, if along with the prayer there be not the cherished desire after holiness, and the perpetual effort to abhor—*to abhor*—that which is evil, and cleave to that which is good.

8

CHRISTIAN JOY

Rejoice in the Lord alway! and again I say rejoice. PHILIP-
PIANS 4:4

A PERSON who reads this letter of Paul to the Philippian Christians
will hardly fail to observe, how often the apostle speaks of joy; how
often he alludes to his own sources of joy; how often he bids his
brethren to rejoice. There must be significance in this. The apostle
Paul was not a man to use many words without meaning; and that
divine Spirit, that guided him in what he wrote, never speaks for
naught. When we read again and again injunctions like this, "Finally
my brethren rejoice in the Lord," or "in all things by prayer and supplication *with thanksgiving,* make your requests known," etc.; or when
he says, "for your furtherance and *joy* of faith," "that your *rejoicing*
may be more abundant," "I joy and rejoice with you all; for this cause
also do ye joy and rejoice with me"; or, in the text, bids them "rejoice
in the Lord alway," repeating the injunction with unusual and very
marked emphasis, "and again I say, rejoice"—when we read all these
passages and more than these, in one very brief letter, we may be
assured that the writer was very earnest in his own rejoicing, and was
quite anxious that his brethren should rejoice too, and was certain
that they had ample cause of rejoicing.

It is well too to observe what was the condition of him who thus
constantly tells of joyfulness, and what the condition of those upon
whom he urged the duty of rejoicing and thankfulness. When Paul
wrote to the Christians at Philippi, he was a prisoner at Rome; liable
not merely to be tried upon the accusations made against him by the
Jews (which were not likely to condemn him), but liable also to
punishment for preaching a new religion which was not tolerated by
the laws of the state, and more especially since it had a direct tendency
to break down the religion of the state. He knew all this—he knew
that his life was in danger; and yet still he rejoices, for he is confident
that whether by his life or his death, Christ will be glorified, and he

feels that to him (as he says) "to live is Christ, and to die, gain." He can rejoice too that his imprisonment has been the means of drawing attention to the religion he preaches, and that many have waxed bolder in preaching the gospel by reason of his bonds.

And thus he, who was a prisoner, and could not know his fate, yet found abundant matter of thankfulness and rejoicing. The Philippian Christians, to whom he wrote, had to bear more than ordinary trials. The apostle himself, when first preaching there, had been grievously mistreated; and the zeal and hatred of the Jews had made them continue to wage an unremitting warfare against the few disciples there of the true faith. They had adversaries, they had opposition, they had persecutions. Yet Paul says, "rejoice." Surely, then, when we see an apostle rejoicing in bonds, and again and again saying "rejoice" to a feeble body of injured and persecuted men, we may know that thanksgiving and rejoicing is a great Christian duty, and an exalted Christian privilege. Therefore, I desire to speak now of *Christian thankfulness* and Christian joy.

An unthankful and complaining spirit is an abiding sin against God, and a cause of almost continual unhappiness; and yet how common such a spirit is. How prone we seem to be to forget the good that life knows, and remember and brood over its evil—to forget its joys, and think only of its sorrows—to forget thankfulness, and remember only to complain. The ox will graze all day in green pastures, and know of nothing but the moment's enjoyment; and many a man will enjoy the blessings that are so spread out before him, the pleasures that are so thickly strewed along his path, and never have one moment's thought of the bountiful Being that gave them, that good and gracious One who is "kind to the unthankful and the evil." But then let trouble come—want or suffering, disappointment or anxiety, remorse or dread, and how soon he grows dissatisfied with life, how soon he complains of his hard lot, and murmurs against the God that made him.

Is it not lamentable that men will never thank God for the countless blessings he confers upon them, and then remember him only to complain of the evils which they have brought upon themselves, and which are never half so great as their misconduct deserves? And if in those who care nothing for him that made them and preserves and blesses them, those who neglect or hate him, this conduct is so strange, how is it with those who have yet more to thank God for, who are his children by the new and spiritual birth, who are made heirs of God, and joint heirs with Jesus Christ? And yet, my brethren, how many an earnest Christian is grievously wanting in thankfulness for his

Heavenly Father's goodness, and suffers himself often to complain and be peevish and fretful at the little trials of life; forgetting how much more there is even in the midst of trials, how much more joy than sorrow in his lot, and forgetting too the command of him who has said, "In every thing give thanks." We need to watch and pray concerning this disposition. We need to strive to change our ways of thinking and feeling about it. Let a man be reminded of the many blessings God had given him, and he will say at once, "Ah, but this one trouble destroys all my happiness, mars all my enjoyment"—and he will turn away his eyes from everything pleasant around him, and gaze moodily or fretfully at this source of trouble. If he does not carry it so far as this, he will be sure to let this discomfort prevent all thankfulness. Now I say we need to change here. Our feeling ought to be, that though we have troubles, yet these shall not prevent our being glad and thankful at the many blessings, the more numerous and rich and undeserved blessings we enjoy. "In every thing give thanks." Thank God for your enjoyments—they are the gift of his goodness.

Do you really, my Christian hearer, look upon the blessings, I mean the *temporal* blessings, you enjoy as the gift of God? Do you really thank him with the heart, even when your lips are uttering words of thankfulness? My brethren, I have sometimes feared that with many of us there is three times a day a solemn mockery practiced. How often it happens that a family gather time after time around their table, spread with that abundant and pleasing food which, in the good providence of God they have been enabled to provide, and seem to thank their Heavenly Father for these blessings, and yet they do not thank him—and yet no heart of all those gathered there feels one emotion of gratitude to God. The grace before meals is necessary and proper, they believe, but neither he that speaks again nor they that hear again the oft-repeated words have any real feeling of thankfulness at all. I do not say this is so with all—I do not say it is always so with any; but is it not too often so? And if here, when you are professing to give thanks, you feel no thankfulness, alas how must it be in those unnumbered hours when you neither think nor speak of gratitude.

I say then that with reference to temporal blessings, to earthly good, to the ordinary course of affairs in life I fear you are sadly lacking, my Christian brethren, in the gratitude to God which you ought to cultivate and cherish. It is a poor return to make for that goodness which crowns your life with so many blessings, to be complaining constantly because something goes wrong. You say to a child who complains of what is given him, that he ought to be glad it is so good; it is far better than he deserves. And so might it be said to every professed child of God—however few comparatively may be your advantages and however many comparatively your troubles, you ought to be thankful it is no worse, you ought to remember that it is far better than you deserve.

But the rejoicing contemplated by the text amounts to very much more than gratitude for temporal mercies. Indeed, ample as I have tried to show is the ground for gratitude on the score of earthly blessings, and sadly remiss as we are in that we do not cultivate more of the spirit of thankfulness for present good, yet all these are at last but our Father's meaner gifts, and all such sources of pleasure are as nothing when compared with that higher rejoicing to which the Christian is here invited. It is to rejoice on account of *spiritual* blessings.

I know that in calling upon Christians to rejoice over their religious privileges and blessings, one is met by the danger of *spiritual pride*. I remember the Pharisee, who thanked God (at least he said he did—I doubt if he did really feel any thankfulness at all) that he was better than other men. I have not forgotten how sinful a feeling like this must be—how unworthy of creatures such as we are, who have no good in us, whose righteousness must be altogether the gift of another. This very consideration is sufficient to counteract every tendency to spiritual pride. If a man really is a Christian, he knows that all the good in him is of God; he knows that he has to thank God for every privilege he enjoys, and he cannot deserve credit for that which is the gift of another—and his gratitude to the giver would better make him humble than proud. No, the true Christian may rejoice over what the Lord has made him, without forgetting that he owes it to the Lord—"by the grace of God I am what I am." In the world, the proudest men are commonly those who have least to be proud of, and so in religion the man who has much of it is in very little danger of being proud thereof, for that religion whose essence is humility will always teach him to "rejoice with trembling."

I repeat then that the text looks properly to a spiritual rejoicing, and on the score of spiritual blessings. There are many reasons why Christians should rejoice, should rejoice in the Lord. Here are some of them.

I bid you rejoice, my dear hearer, because you have at least been awakened to a sense of your sins—that you are not a careless, nor a hardened sinner. It is a good thing for a man to be aware of his condition, because he is then more likely to seek relief. If a man finds he is in danger, there is hope that he will strive to escape. If one knows that he is diseased, and feels it, there is hope that he will seek the physician. And the fact that a man feels that he is a sinner shows that he is beginning to have more correct ideas of what sin is, and what holiness is, of what is his own character, and what that character ought to be. An awakened sinner is no more free from sin than he was before. But then he is more likely to seek the Saviour and thus be forgiven and purified. An old writer has said that a bucket which is being drawn out of the well is not felt to be heavy, till it begins to rise out of the water; that a man who is under water does not feel the weight of the tons that may be above him, so much as he would feel the weight of one little tubful of water on his head when he is out. So when a man feels the weight of his sin it seems as if he is not so wholly immersed in sin as he was before; he is coming out of it.

It is a lamentable thing that so many men and women are living without seeming ever to think of their being sinners. They not only enjoy God's bounty without ever thanking him, but they incur his displeasure without fearing him, they heap up for themselves wrath against the day of wrath without taking time to think what they are doing. Do you want to find the most lamentable, the most pitiable and deplorable spectacle on earth? Do not tell me of one who thinks he will soon recover and live many years, when consumption has fastened its grasp upon him and tomorrow he must die. Do not tell me of him who sails gaily down the quickening current and forgets the cataract that is before him. But come and look upon the careless and reckless sinner, who is going on without one moment's thought to eternal death; who is standing upon the slippery places of earthly life, while the fiery billows of death and perdition roll beneath his feet, and yet does not seem to know where he is; who has in truth nothing before him but a certain fearful looking for of judgment and fiery indignation which shall devour the adversaries, and yet moves on as if the present were all bright and he had nothing to fear. But there is the *hardened* sinner—who has eyes that seeing see not, and ears that hearing hear not—who hardened the heart till now nothing can move, till God's wrath cannot alarm, nor his love attract, till his threatenings and his invitations fall alike unheeded on the ear, till the story of the bleeding, dying love of Jesus can never move. Oh, may God in his mercy deliver you, my dear hearer, from being a *hardened sinner!* Whatever else befall you, God forbid that you should be a hardened sinner! And my brethren I say I rejoice, and I bid you rejoice, that you are at least awakened—that you are not careless, not hardened.

But there is greater cause still for rejoicing. My Christian brother, can you not rejoice that you have faith in Christ and enjoyment of religion, communion with God and hope of glory? You have faith in Christ. You have found him of whom Moses in the law and the prophets did write. You have found him who was exalted a Prince and a Saviour, to give repentance unto Israel and remission of sins. You have found him who was lifted up to draw all men unto him. You know him who is the chief among ten thousand and altogether lovely. You have traced out something of the unsearchable riches of Christ. You have found the hidden treasure, the pearl of great price. You have learned that there is balm in Gilead, that there is a great Physician there; he has checked your fearful, mortal malady, and you shall live. You have looked to the brazen serpent, you are healed. You have sprinkled your doorpost with the blood of God's atoning Lamb, and the angel of destruction will pass you by. You have fled to the city of refuge, and the destroyer cannot come near you. You have laid your sins by faith on your substitute and he has borne them away into the wilderness. You have bathed in the fountain that was opened in the house of King David for sin and for uncleanness, and the defilement of guilt has been washed away. You have brought to Jesus the writing that bound you as a servant of sin, and he has annulled it by nailing it to his cross.

In a word, you believe on the Saviour, and to you that believe he is precious. And my brother, if all these things be true of you, if Jesus is yours and you are his, have you not cause for rejoicing and praise and thanksgiving and love? We are told that on one occasion the disciples whom Jesus had sent out, returned with rejoicing, saying, "Lord, even the devils are subject to us through thy name." And the Master replied, "Rejoice not in this, that the devils are subject unto you, but rather rejoice that your names are written in heaven." And, my brethren, if you be true believers in Jesus, you may well rejoice that your names are written in heaven. It may amount to but little that your names are written on an earthly record as Christians, for that does not prove it true; a man may have a name to live and be dead. But if they are written in that blessed book, the Lamb's book of life, then may you rejoice indeed.

Again, you have the enjoyment of religious privileges. You have within your reach continually those delights which religion alone can afford. You can feed on the bread of life which came down from heaven, and drink sweet draughts from the wellspring of salvation. You can read the blessed teachings of God's holy word, you can walk to the house of God in company with those you love, and hear the sound of the glorious gospel, and rejoice that being mixed with faith in you that hear it, the word preached profits you. You can gather together for united prayer and feel that you sit together in heavenly places in Christ Jesus. You can lift your voices together in hymning the praises of your glorious Redeemer. And is there not in privileges like these matter for great and continual rejoicing?

Then you can enjoy communion with God. My hearer, have you ever felt what is meant by communion with God? Or is it only a something you have read of in the Bible and heard of from the pulpit, without understanding it? If you be a real, earnest Christian, you have felt what it is. You are able to call God Father. Although by sin men are separated from him and can look to him only as an offended Lord and a righteously angry Judge, yet you may rejoice at knowing that you have been adopted into the household of faith, and have received that spirit of adoption whereby you cry, "Abba, Father," and can in humble faith and earnest confidence lift your prayer unto him who is our Father in heaven. You can pray without ceasing unto him. As you hunger and thirst after righteousness, you can go to him and know that you shall be filled. As you feel yourself weak, you can hope for strength from him.

It is especially a privilege to pray to him alone, to commune with him in secret—to enter into your closet and shut the door and pray to your Father which is in secret, as knowing that your Father which seeth in secret himself shall reward you openly. You can pour out there before him your heart's inmost sorrows, your spirit's own peculiar wants. You can wrestle there alone with your God, for the blessings you need, and know that asking you shall receive. You can confess every sin, of word or deed, of thought or desire, and ask for forgiveness through the Saviour in whom you trust. You can pour out your soul there in earnest supplication for those you love who love not Jesus; you can spread out all their sad case before your God, and implore him to stop them and turn them and rescue and save them. Oh, the privilege of private prayer, the joy and peace that flow to the true believer from personal, spiritual communion with the Father of his spirit!

But there is not only faith in the Saviour, and the enjoyment of religious privileges, and communion with God, but as if these were not enough to make the heart overflow with joy, we have more—there is the hope of glory. It is a bright and beautiful change when the water of some little muddy pool is drunk up by the sun, leaving behind all its earthly defilements, and when it appears again in raindrops is clothed, as the sunbeams shine through it, in all the bright hues of the rainbow. But this is nothing, compared with the change from a sin-defiled dweller on the earth, to a glorified inmate of the Paradise of God. How blessed will be that change! when they who have entered the strait gate and walked the narrow way through the troubles and trials of earth, shall pass through the pearly gates and tread the golden streets of the New Jerusalem, the glorious city of our God; when they who have groaned in sickness and sighed in sorrow, they who have languished in pain and borne the agony of death, shall pass into that blest abode where "sickness and sorrow, pain and death, are felt and feared no more." Christian brother, I bid you read humbly, and yet rejoicingly, the soul-inspiring descriptions which are given us in the book of Revelation—the descriptions of the glorious city, the river and the tree of life, the robes of white, the harps of gold, the chorus of redeemed spirits, the song of Moses and the Lamb—I cannot tell what all these mean, but I know they mean and are intended to mean, all that is glorious and gladdening and bright and beautiful. Read it, humbly and thankfully, and let your heart swell with devout rejoicing, and your bosom heave with humble gratitude to him who has "given us everlasting consolation and good hope through grace," the hope of immortality and eternal life, the hope of heaven, the hope of glory.

Happy art thou, O Christian, if such joys, such privileges, such cheering, gladdening hopes, are indeed experienced. How much our Heavenly Father has given you of temporal good, how much more of spiritual enjoyment and soul-sustaining hope. How much the Lord of life and glory has done on your behalf. Go tell one that is able to understand you, of his parents' tenderness and care; of his father's yearning fondness, his mother's unutterable love; of all their anxiety and uneasiness and privation and suffering on his account, and if he is not moved to love and gratitude, you call him a thankless wretch. Has not God loved *you* with more than a father's, more than a mother's love? Has not Jesus suffered for you unspeakable anguish and agony, has he not died for you? Will you be thankful for all goodness and mercy? When he, who has done so much for you, who has given you all those exalted privileges and blessed joys and glorious hopes on which we have been dwelling, when he bids you rejoice in him, *rejoice* always in him. Cultivate a spirit of thanksgiving, a spirit of rejoicing, and devote your life to his service, that all your life should be one ceaseless song of joy, one constant hymn of praise, "to him that loved us, and washed us from our sins in his own blood, and hath made us kings and priests unto God and his Father!" "Finally, brethren, rejoice in the Lord."

9

THE RESURRECTION OF OUR LORD

The Lord is risen indeed. LUKE 24:34

VERY near the place of the crucifixion there was a garden belonging to Joseph, of Arimathaea, this being the name of a little country town from which he had come. He was a man of wealth, as no other could have owned a garden just outside the walls of a great city. He, too, was a man of elevated social position: for excepting the high priest there was no higher position possible for a Jew than to be a member of the Sanhedrin. He was a disciple of Jesus, but "secretly, for fear of the Jews." It is difficult to interpret that expression with certainty, but it gives us a rather painful view of the powerful influence exerted upon the religion of many men by social considerations. This gentleman was afraid of losing social caste, and afraid of losing a distinguished position, and so he had not been able to declare himself a disciple of Jesus before the world.

In the Sanhedrin Joseph appears to have opposed the vote by which Jesus was condemned, and we may suppose that from this garden of his, near to the place, he had looked out with mournful interest upon the scene of the crucifixion. Perhaps as his eye wandered, it fell upon the new tomb which he had caused to be cut out from the solid rock in the garden, preparing it for the entombment of himself and his household, but in which no one had yet been laid. It occurred to him that he would honor the prophet, the crucified, by making him the first to be buried in his new tomb. It is one of the contradictions that are perpetually occurring in our Lord's life; that he died as a despised malefactor, and yet he was buried like a man of the greatest distinction. There was need of haste after his death occurred, for that was three o'clock, and if they waited until the sun went down and the Sabbath began it would be impossible, so Joseph hurried to the Roman governor and asked permission to bury the prophet in his tomb. Pilate thought it unusual that he should have died so soon, since those crucified usually lingered for a day or two, sometimes for several days. But all the sleepless suffering of the night before and the dark mysterious agony of the day had told rapidly upon him; thus in six hours he had died. Pilate sent an officer to ascertain the fact, and upon his report, he gave the permission required. Joseph hurried to buy costly ointment to embalm the body. Another member of the Sanhedrin, Nicodemus, who three years before had visited Jesus by night, also went to Golgotha. No expense was spared by those distinguished and wealthy men in expressing love and admiration for the body of the prophet. I wonder if Nicodemus did not remember, as he and the attendants took down the body of Christ, how he had said to him at that night interview: "As Moses lifted up the serpent in the wilderness, even so shall the Son of Man be lifted up: that whosoever believeth on him should not perish but have everlasting life."

This interment was witnessed, we are told, by two women—Mary Magdalene, and another Mary, the mother of Joseph. They stood at a distance and so did not see that Nicodemus had brought those spices. Now as the sun was going down, and the stone was rolled to the mouth of the sepulcher, the women went to the city planning what they would do when the Sabbath was passed. So the night came and the morning. Those were very weary hours of that Sabbath day for the disciples of Jesus; there never was amid all the crushed hopes of human hearts on earth an experience so bitter as theirs. They had "trusted that it had been he who should have redeemed Israel," they climbed up to the hope that he was the promised Messiah, and now it was all gone. His enemies, to be sure, had heard a whisper from some source that he had predicted that he would be crucified, and that he would rise again on the third day. They seized upon that idea, and went to work to make sure that nothing should be done by his friends to simulate a resurrection. And make sure they did! They got a guard of Roman soldiers to watch the tomb, whose lives would be the forfeit if they neglected their duty. They put upon the stone before the door the seal of the Roman government which it was death for any man to break. They made their work sure.

They remembered the prediction, and why did not the disciples remember it, too? Well, I suppose they had never looked upon the prediction as representing a reality. When Peter and James and John came down with him from the mount of transfiguration and he told them they must tell no man what they had seen on the mount, until the Son of Man was risen from the dead, we are told that they used to question and reason with one another as to what the rising from the dead meant. Why, it could not mean a literal rising from the dead.

King Messiah was not going to be crucified, and come to life—of course, it could not mean that. It was contrary to all their ideas. And as it could not mean a literal rising from the dead, what could it mean? I suppose the idea of a real death and a real resurrection never entered their minds; therefore they did not remember it, because it had never been reality to their thought.

The hours went on, and when the sun set on the Jewish Sabbath, which was Saturday evening, the women went to the shops, which were opened at sunset, to buy their spices. Some of these women had been accustomed to contribute of their substance for the support of Jesus and his followers, and they were going now to make their last contribution to do some honor to his dead body. When the early morning came, they went to the tomb. On their way there occurred to their minds a difficulty. The two women had observed that it was a very large stone that was rolled against the tomb, and it occurred to them that they would not be able to remove it. But they pressed on, and when they arrived at the sepulcher—the stone was rolled away. Immediately the thought came, not that he was risen, but that the body had been removed by some friend or some enemy. So one of them, Mary Magdalene, rushed back to the city to the residence of John, where Peter also was, to tell them about it. The other woman remained. And presently looking into the sepulcher they saw two angels, who spoke to them and said: "Why seek ye the living among the dead? He is not here, he is risen. Go tell his disciples that he is leading the way to Galilee and they shall see him there." So they departed to carry this message. I fancy they went to Bethany. Most likely the nine disciples, who were accustomed to go to Bethany every night with the Master, had gone there now.

Soon after the women left, here came Peter and John, eagerly hastening at the news which Mary had brought that the sepulcher was opened. John came first, and stopped and looked in, but in his deeply reverential way did not enter. Then Peter came, and, bold as he always was, rushed right in and John followed him. They saw the linen cloths that had wrapped the body lying, and the napkin which had been wrapped about the head was folded and laid apart. John telling the story afterward, says that he "saw, and believed." Those accustomed to dealing with evidence know that among matters of importance, very slight circumstances will sometimes clinch the whole thing and leave no doubt about it. Here was such a slight circumstance. It could not be that friends had borne that body away, for they would have carried it away with the cloths; and enemies would not have left the cloths folded and neatly laid away. Their presence there and the tokens of order and loving care satisfied John that the Master was risen indeed. No doubt there came back upon him a recollection of those forgotten sayings of the Master, and he now saw what he could not understand when he came down from the mount of transfiguration, what the rising from the dead did mean. It meant reality. He saw and believed.

But Jesus was not there, and they knew not what to do nor to think, and so they went soon away. However, Mary Magdalene had followed them to the tomb, and was now standing without and weeping. After a little she stooped timidly and looked into the tomb, and again the angels appeared and said, "Woman, why weepest thou?" Still she had no thought that he was risen. She said, "They have taken away my Lord, and I know not where they have laid him." Then she turned around and through her tears saw a man standing by, who she took it for granted was in charge of the garden, and she said, "Sir, if thou has borne him away, please tell me where thou hast laid him?"

Do you remember what followed? Ah! she heard a voice, a voice that years before had spoken and the dread demons that possessed her fled away; a voice from which she had heard so often such wise and loving words as thrilled her soul and would linger forever in her memory. She heard that voice as he said, "Mary." And she turned and said, "My teacher!" I do not know exactly what is meant by the words our Lord then spoke. They are obscure, but I think they mean this; that with the superstition which was common to the Jews—and these disciples had a great many such erroneous notions and retained them for a great while—they were likely to say among themselves, "Ah: but it is just his ghost, he has gone to the Father." The disciples thought the same thing when he appeared to them that evening. The brethren at Mary's house thought that when Peter appeared for whom they were praying in prison; they said it was his spirit. It seems that Mary feared he had ascended and this was only a phantom, and so she was about to lay hold of him to settle that point, when he said, "Touch me not: for I have not yet ascended to my Father; but go to my brethren and say unto them, I ascend unto my Father and your Father, and to my God and your God." So she turned away to fulfill the mission.

Sometime after, Jesus appeared to the other women and gave them commissions with his own lips likewise. As the morning went on these women told their story, and the disciples would not hear a word of it. They seemed to be strangely incredulous. They said it was all idle tales. With that magnificent, supercilious superiority with which men often speak as regards women, they said it was all women's idle tales. Does it seem strange and sad that they were incredulous? I am glad of it, for as an old writer has said, "They doubted, that we might not doubt." You can see that these men were not credulous enthusiasts, seizing without solid evidence upon something they wanted to believe. They had forgotten the whole idea of a resurrection of Jesus, though their enemies believed it. Moreover, when the story was now told them, it was idle tales. And so there came more evidence that broke down all their unbelief, and left no doubt for them, and leaves no doubt for us.

As the day went on, our Lord appeared to Simon Peter, not to condemn him, but as a condescension to poor fallen Simon, because he had fallen so low. The loving Lord would not allow him to go away in despair, he appeared to him. Then in the afternoon, he came to two men walking toward Emmaus, talking sorrowfully together. They had believed that this Jesus of Nazareth was the Redeemer of Israel and now that belief was all gone. Then they had heard tales that some women had seen visions of angels and said he was alive, and men had been there and the tomb was empty. They did not know what to think of it, but they talked it over very sadly and confusedly.

What a scene it was when suddenly there stepped in a quiet man and addressed them. He asked them what they were talking about, and they spoke with sad faces and then went on the colloquy with which you are familiar. What a scene it was when he began to open to them the predictions! He was not only conqueror and king, but sufferer and sacrifice, and the very words burned within them as they received new light about the Messiah and began to see that possibly he might be crucified. Perhaps then the story of the women that he was risen was not an idle tale. What a scene it was when breaking bread their eyes were opened and they knew him, but for one brief moment, and he vanished from their sight. Then as they came back to Jerusalem, they said the Lord had risen indeed and had appeared to Simon and they told their story.

As they talked about it with the doors shut for fear of the Jews, suddenly he stood in their room and in his old loving way he said, "Peace be unto you." But they had that same Jewish superstition. They could not believe it was reality. They thought he was dead and this was his ghost, and felt the thrill that men feel at the very idea of seeing something supernatural. And he said "Why are ye troubled? See, it is not a spirit! Look at the wounds in the hands and in the side? Give me food. They gave him food, and he ate it before them." Their incredulity broke down. It had to break down, then and there. They had been told that the Messiah was to be despised and rejected and to die and to rise again. There was nothing hard to believe about it if they understood the Scriptures, but the fact came first and they were obliged to believe the fact. Then their hearts were opened to see that the fact had been predicted long before by the prophets.

We have reached the Lord's day evening. You remember how a week later he overcame the incredibility of Thomas, how he appeared in Galilee and then back in Jerusalem and at length in the presence of the disciples ascended into heaven. Without following those appearances I wish to make certain observations respecting the resurrection of the Son of Man, even the resurrection of Jesus Christ as an unquestionable reality.

My friends, if I do not know that Jesus Christ rose from the dead then this world has no history. I do not know anything in the past if I do not know that. If a man will look carefully and thoughtfully over all these evidences, will note the slowness of belief of these men, their intelligence, will see that they were not prejudiced enthusiasts, will see how when they had fairly been convinced of this they gave their lives for it, if a man will put all circumstances together including the traditions and discrepancies of the experience, I am satisfied that he will see, if he is willing to see, that the fact shines out clearly. I will not say a man is obliged to believe it. If a man is determined to doubt he can always find some loophole for doubt, but a man who is desirous of believing will see that it is reality: that there is no excuse for question.

The second observation is that the resurrection of the Lord Jesus establishes the truth of Christianity. The apostle Paul says he is declared to be the Son of God by the resurrection from the dead. Now Lazarus was raised from the dead and that did not prove such a thing concerning him; but Jesus of Nazareth had claimed to be the Son of God, had claimed it before the Sanhedrin when he had been denounced as a blasphemer, and after all his high claims and predictions if he had not been all that he claimed there never would have been such a high destiny accomplished for him. It was the sign manual of the Deity, it was the seal of the Sovereign of the Universe affixed to his claim, it declared him to be all that he had ever professed to be, and so it establishes the truth of all his teachings and the truth of the whole Christian society. The great fact that Jesus Christ rose from the dead is the central fact of the evidence of Christianity.

The third observation is that the resurrection of Christ consummated his work of redemption. This is a view which I think does not appear to come often within the sight of Christian teachers at the present time, and yet was much in the minds of the first disciples. The resurrection with them was not merely a great fact that established the truth of Christianity but also consummated the work of redemption. Paul says, "Who was delivered for our offenses and was raised again for our justification." He says to the Corinthians, "And that he died for all, that they which live should not henceforth live unto themselves, but unto him which died for them, and rose again." He says not merely "died for them" but that he "rose again." He laid down his life, and took it again for us. He rose triumphant over death and over sin and over Satan in our behalf. And thus you see how it is that in the Epistle to the Romans he makes this statement: "If thou shalt confess with thy mouth the Lord Jesus, and shalt believe in thine heart that God hath raised him from the dead, thou shalt be saved." That is the consummation of the Christian redemption, believe that God raised him from the dead and confess him with the mouth, and you shall be saved.

The fourth observation is that the resurrection of Christ is the pledge of the resurrection of his people. "Now is Christ risen from the dead and become the first fruits of them that slept." The sheaf of barley that they weighed as the first fruits of the harvest was regarded as a pledge that the rest of the harvest would come in its time and Christ's resurrection is the first fruits, the pledge of our resurrection. And so the apostle wrote to the Thessalonians, "But I would not have you to be ignorant, brethren, concerning them which are asleep, that ye sorrow not, even as others which have no hope." A great poem before that time had expressed it, "When a man has once died there is no resurrection," but Paul says, "If we believe that Jesus died and rose again, even so them also which sleep in Jesus will God bring with him." The resurrection of Christ is the pledge, I say, of the resurrection of his people.

Yet a fifth observation. The resurrection of Christ is celebrated by us on the Lord's day. I have no time to go into the argument which is here involved, but we believe from slight intimations in the Acts of the Apostles and in Revelation which show conclusively that the Christians of that time held religious meetings on the first day of the week, and from the light which is shed back upon it, and from known facts we learn that the apostles had authorized that the Sabbath should be transferred to the first day of the week; not that there were any minute directions, such as Moses had given to the Jews, that they should pick up sticks and make fires on the Sabbath day; not that there were any directions as to ceremonial but they were reminded the old primeval Sabbath which God had declared should be kept holy to him. Those directions stand without any specific qualifications as to how we shall do them and stand with new significance in that they represent the resurrection of Christ—a day concerning which we have no specific details as to how we are to observe it, but the general thought that it is the old day of God which is to be set apart from all other days and sanctified to him and also the day that represents the resurrection of Christ.

Finally, the resurrection of the Lord Jesus is a pledge to his people to live a risen life. You remember what the apostle says to the Romans: "Know ye not that so many of us as were baptized into Jesus were baptized into his death; therefore we were buried with him by baptism into death, and, like as Christ was raised from the dead by the glory of the Father even so we also should walk in the newness of life." Oh, ye Christian people, when you first set out in Christ's service, you did by a solemn ceremony declare that by faith in Jesus Christ you had died to sin and risen to a new life and were going to live always afterward a new life. Has it been so with you? Does your heart smite you with the painful thought that it has been but very partially so? O friends and brethren, then God has given you a time to set out afresh.

10

NECESSITY OF THE ATONEMENT

The blood of Jesus Christ his Son cleanseth from all sin.
I John 1:7

My hearers, what is the most wonderful event that ever occurred on earth, that ever happened in the universe? The history of our race is so full of wonderful events—you might well pause for your answer. My answer would be this: by far the most wonderful thing that has ever happened in the universe, is the atoning death of Jesus Christ the Lord. If without philosophizing, if in simplicity you will take what God's Word declares concerning it, you will not only see this to be so, perhaps you will feel it to be so. If you will remember who he was —the thought would startle us if we were not so used to it—if you will remember how he died, how the Lord of life and glory, the sinless one, how he died in suffering and shame, and above all if you will remember what he died for, what his death is declared in the Scriptures to mean for the universe and for us, then you will believe that this is the great wonder of all wonders. And yet, God be thanked, it may be the simplest matter of each individual human heart's everyday experience to rest upon that wonderful thought. There are many things we can never comprehend as to their nature, which are yet unquestionable as facts and essential to our existence. To declare before heaven and earth that all our hopes are turned upon the atoning death of Jesus Christ, a man may do that, may live on that atoning death, although it be a mystery he cannot solve.

I wish to speak today of the atonement of Jesus Christ. But that is a large theme. I wish to speak of one particular aspect of it, of the *necessity* of an atonement by the propitiatory death of Jesus Christ. Though the theme looks abstract at the outset, and may be uninviting, I pray your diligent heed, for we are dealing with the substance of the gospel.

The thought of our age turns itself against this necessity of the atonement to a great extent. Many of the tendencies of our time incline men to question whether there is any virtue in sacrificial atonement for sin, and there is nothing more common than to hear superficial people, even good people, saying that they do not see how God the Heavenly Father of men should not forgive us, just as we earthly fathers forgive our children, without requiring some great provision as the basis of this forgiveness. After all, we can learn on such a subject as this only from the Bible. Men in all ages have for the most part recognized the necessity of an atonement. They have shown their recognition of it in very distorted forms, often they have had grossly erroneous conceptions of deity and of their relations to deity. Their ideas of sacrifice and propitiation have been sadly erroneous, grotesque sometimes, often horrible, always degrading. But these are but distortions of a true and right sentiment, of which the human soul is conscious. And then God's Word comes to confirm this instinctive persuasion that there is need of an atonement. The idea of propitiation and of sacrifice which all nations have had finds its counterpart in the divine Word. In the Jewish purifications and the Jewish sacrifices there was not really made an atonement for sin, but they signified an atonement for sin which did not then exist, they pointed forward to an atonement for sin in the future which God was to accomplish. And now for us that something future has come and the true atonement which all these things prefigured has been fully explained in the complete Word of God. In the light of the New Testament facts and under the guidance of New Testament ideas the necessity of an atonement may be practically clear to our minds. Two chief points are to be distinguished, the *priest* and the *sacrifice*.

1. First, the priest. According to the Old Testament conception of propitiation, certain men were separated from their fellow men and made mediators between men and God. Now the New Testament counterpart of that idea of propitiation gives us two senses in which the word "priest" may be considered. In one sense there is but one priest, Jesus Christ; in another sense all Christian people are priests, and all equally. In one sense, I say, the New Testament counterpart is that the only priest is Jesus Christ. So we have for the New Testament economy the atoning and interceding word of Jesus Christ. "Seeing then that we have a great High Priest, that is passed through the heavens, Jesus the Son of God, let us hold fast our profession." As the Jewish high priest went through the veil into the most holy place and offered sacrifice, so our High Priest has passed through the heavens into the true sanctuary of that eternal world. His sacrifice is not the blood of bulls and of goats which could never take away sin, which could only symbolize and represent the idea of atonement,

his sacrifice is his own blood; himself the High Priest and himself the Lamb of God which taketh away the sin of the world. Not only has he begun this work for the atoning of men, but he lives ever the same High Priest, not dying like the Jewish priest and turning over his work to others but by his continual intercession "he is able to save to the utmost them that come to God through him, seeing he ever liveth to make intercession for them." In that sense the whole conception of a propitiation centers upon the propitiation of the Lord Jesus Christ, there is no other priest. No one must come between that priest and our souls.

Will you pardon me an incident that at this moment comes back to my mind. Some years ago, as I was starting to come to New York, a gentleman came up and said, "I want to introduce you to two young ladies. I want to put them under your charge." He explained that some very kind persons in Baltimore were providing for the education of the girls whose families were refined but were now without means. So I brought them along in my care. I knew where they were going—they were going to a convent school. Before parting from them I thought it right to say this much at least—one was an Episcopalian and the other a Presbyterian—I said, "Now whatever ideas you may get in going away, try to cling to the thought that nobody shall come between you and Jesus Christ; you do not need anybody between you and him, try to cling to the idea that you will not have anyone between you and him." One of them said, "Of course not, because that would be a Roman Catholic notion, wouldn't it?" Alas! one of them is a Roman Catholic today and the other was carried home, I understood, to prevent it. I have no word of bitterness for the persons who believe and honestly teach those things, but it seems to me that their teachings strike at the heart of the gospel, and that I must say without reserve there is but one priest, Jesus Christ himself, and nobody has any business to come between my soul and him.

In another sense you are all priests, all alike. Alas! for the fact that so many of those whom we call Protestants have revived the Old Testament idea of human priests, set apart from their fellow men, and even call the New Testament minister a priest. The idea to which the human heart is so inclined is that the propitiation of Jesus Christ is not enough for us poor souls, and we must have some fellow man to be a mediator between us and God, to make expiation for our sins. I am glad to get anybody to pray for me, but I want no prayers of a so-called priest more than of any other man. No official station according to the New Testament idea gives a man's prayers more efficacy than they would have without the official station. A man's piety is more effective than his position. How ready people are to think that the minister's prayers, even where they don't call him priest, have a peculiar efficacy. According to the New Testament conception there is in one sense, then, but one high priest and we need no other, and in another sense we are all alike high priests to offer up spiritual sacrifices for ourselves and one another.

2. Turn now to the other conception, the conception of sacrifice; what does that mean in the light of the New Testament? It may be regarded in various ways.

(a) The sacrificial death of the Redeemer is in one sense a ransom for sinful man, a redemption, a purchase of his salvation. It is the idea of buying and selling, but especially the idea of ransoming from captivity. "Jesus paid it all," the little child of today gets hold of the thought

> Jesus paid it all,
>   All the debt I owe.
> Jesus died and paid it all,
>   Yes, all the debt I owe.

This is a very familiar thought to human experience, and it often comes home to us in simple forms. I am in debt, and all the debt I owe, Jesus paid it. I am a captive, I am a bondman, Jesus died to ransom me. You must not press the idea too far or you will be misled. But within limits it is just and instructive. We are bound captives, and Jesus is our ransom. He purchased our salvation.

(b) Again, the atoning death of Jesus Christ propitiates God. It makes God favorably inclined toward us. It makes God propitious toward those with whom for their sins he must otherwise be angry. It is a very common notion today that anger is wrong: that it is out of the question to speak of God as really feeling anger, and that must be in Scripture a mere figure of speech. But my friends, anger is right sometimes, anger is sometimes necessary. I would not give much for a man who is not sometimes thoroughly angry. A man that knows not how to burn with moral indignation at the wickedness he sees around him and the wrongdoing, there is something wrong in him. Anger is compatible with love. Parents are often angry with their children and yet love them all the time. We find that the apostle knew that it was possible to be angry, and sin not. Anger, I say, is compatible with love. It is altogether a mistake to suppose that anger is always wrong. It is a mistake to think you should not punish a child when you are angry. What was anger given you for but to stimulate you to punish when you should? Because anger is often carried to excess it does not follow that it is all wrong, but it follows that you must control it.

The whole thing is illustrated by the example of our Saviour, who was one day surrounded by a crowd of the unsympathizing and unbelieving, and it is said that he "looked around upon them with anger, being grieved at the hardness of their hearts." That is it, anger and yet grief: grieved and at the same time angry. That is what we need to be: angry and still loving. Anything less than that is a one-sided notion of truth and duty. And that being so, why should men shrink from the thought that God is angry with sin; that he hates sin; that it excites indignation in him, and that something was necessary in order to make God favorable toward sinful beings. Here again we must not press it too far: and we must not press anything too far when dealing with images. It is a gross caricature to say that God the holy Father hates his children and will not be gracious to them until the Redeemer propitiates him into doing what he does not wish to do. The Scriptures tell us he was sent to be the propitiation for our sins because God loved us. Herein is love, not that we loved God, but that he loved us, and sent his Son to be a propitiation for our sins. Yet it is true at the same time that the propitiation was needed because he hated our sins and was angry with them.

(c) Once again, this atoning death of Christ is set before us as necessary to vindicate the right. The most majestic and dignified conception that enters your soul is the conception of moral obligation. There is the word "ought"—"I ought to do this, and ought not to do that." If a man's soul in its deepest fibers responds thrillingly to that sentiment, he has got something in him. The right ought to prevail. Alas! how often, how sadly, how wretchedly, it is otherwise. Our observation of life often leads us to see how wrong goes up and right goes down and we think there ought to be a compensation somehow for such a state of things, under the government of the supreme sovereign, the high and holy God. If our moral nature requires this and cannot be satisfied without some such idea, so does the law of God require it. What propriety is there in having a law if there is to be no punishment for those who violate it? Without some such idea as this the moral government of God would lose its stability. So too there must be something to make it right that God should forgive sin and save the sinner, so that he "may be just," as the Scriptures say he is, "and the justifier of him that believeth in Jesus."

I do not undertake to explain it all; it is a problem that deals with the relations of the finite and the infinite, the relations between sin and holiness, between time and eternity, and if a man thinks he is going to explain and comprehend it in all its relations, of course he deludes himself. If a man is slow to accept it as a fact, until he has it all explained to him he may never accept it. You cannot explain the great fundamental facts of existence, and it is so here. But while not attempting to explain the atonement, we can see how it acts, as a redemption of sin-ruined man, as a propitiation of the holy and sin-hating God, as a vindication of the right. And thus seeing, we rest with satisfaction upon the great fact of the atonement, as revealed in the Scriptures.

There are two great reasons why men do not see the necessity of the atonement; these are inadequate views of sin and inadequate views of God. Let me speak of these. It is a terrible thing for a man to become so familiar with the idea of sin that he says glibly, "I am a sinner," and does not think what it means. It is yet more terrible when he deludes himself into denying the fact. I remember asking a young man who came to see me some years ago if he was a Christian. He answered, "I hardly suppose you would think me one." I said, "If you are not a Christian, you know you are a sinner." "Well," he said, "that depends." Poor sophisticated fellow! When people don't much believe that they are sinners, then it is utterly useless to talk to them about atonement. They see no necessity for it, of course not, if they feel that they personally have no need. Alas! how natural it is for us to have inadequate views of sin. We are so accustomed to it in ourselves and in life all around us. A man says, "Yes, I am a sinner, of course I am, all men are sinners," and that thought that all men are sinners breaks the force of self-condemnations of conscience, and the custom of prevailing immorality weakens our perception of the evil of sin. It is very hard at all times, and especially in an age so inclined to materialism, to have adequate views of sin. It is only in proportion as we realize the evil of sin that we see the necessity of atonement, and on the other hand a hearty recognition of the atonement gives us more adequate views of sin.

The other great reason why men fail to see the need of atonement is that they have inadequate views of God. I am weary of this everlasting talk about God as simply merciful and loving. Weary because that is only one side of the truth. God is not only merciful and loving, God is just. God is holy, and it is quite as needful to appreciate his holiness and his justice as it is to appreciate his love and mercy. My friends, we live in times when a dreamy humanitarianism prevails, when false notions of clemency are perverting the lives of very many well-meaning men. There are people who shrink from the notion of capital punishment, who believe it is wrong to inflict capital punishment for anything. A French writer has well said, "I should be pleased to see capital punishment discontinued, and the sacredness of human life respected, if the murderers will make the beginning." A sentimental pity for criminals may be a very hurtful thing. So likewise we are often told now that children must never be punished in school, and scarcely ever punished by their parents at home. What is to become of us if we give way to these milk-and-water notions, and lose sight of holiness, justice, and right?

But as I have already said, I do not attempt to explain the nature of the atonement. I only wanted to remind you of some of the reasons why, according to the Scriptures, it is necessary that there should be an atonement. If a man says to me, "Do you understand the exact nature of the atoning work of Christ so that you can give me the philosophy of it?" I answer, "No, of course not, but if God is satisfied with the provision he has made, if it is his own provision, and if he proclaims it as sufficient, that is enough for me, and why should not that be enough for you? God says to you and to me, 'The blood of Jesus Christ his Son cleanseth us from all sin.' "

I remember reading a few years ago the story of a party of Hindus, who were traveling along one day, and one of them was stricken down and fell by the way. The other natives looking carelessly at him went along in their selfish fashion, but a missionary stopped by the poor man and kneeling by him said, "What is your hope for eternity? Have you any hope for eternity?" And feebly, with dying breath, the dusky native gasped, "The blood of Jesus Christ cleanseth us from all sin." "Where did you learn that?" the missionary asked. But he could tell no more and died. In the bosom of his garment the missionary found one leaf out of the New Testament in the man's own language, and there were the words that had struck into the soul of the man, the words that had helped him, living and dying—the words of our text today. "The blood of Jesus Christ his Son cleanseth us from all sin."

Ah! my friends, amid all the blessings of this great country, the light of science and the light of literature, amid all the nobleness and real sweetness of what we call culture, amid all the blessedness of Christian homes and Christian society, there is no higher thought for you and me than that uttered to the missionary as he knelt by the poor Hindu's side. Let us take those words as ours for life, and for death, and forever: "The blood of Jesus Christ his Son cleanseth us from all sin."

11

THE SAVIOUR PRAYING FOR US

I pray for them. JOHN 17:9

WE are told in the text of something that Jesus does for us. Do I say rightly that he does for us? He said, "I pray for them," and he was speaking immediately of the little company of men who were right around him, the disciples. On the evening before the crucifixion, at the close of the farewell address, he said, "I pray for them," but you remember how a little later he said, "Neither pray I for these alone, but for them also which shall believe on me through their word; that they all may be one." Through them and their word the circle would widen itself and continue to widen until it should embrace all that should ever become believers on him.

I invite you, dear Christian friends, to take this prayer in the 17th chapter of John, as giving you an idea of what sort of things the Lord Jesus Christ is asking for now in your behalf. Oh, that it may come home to us as downright reality that the Saviour who ever liveth, prays for you and me, knowing us better than we know ourselves, and that such things as these are the things for which he prays.

First then, notice this petition: "I pray not that thou shouldest take them out of the world, but that thou shouldest keep them from the evil." What a common mistake it is among men to think that the only object Jesus Christ has with reference to the human race is to gather a few of them out of this world's destruction and carry them to the better world. But he said, "I pray not that thou shouldest take them out of the world, but that thou shouldest keep them from the evil." He was going out of the world, and his heart longed after those who had been with him. They wondered why they could not go with him, and one even said, in self-confident fervor, "I am ready to go with thee to death." But he said, "I do not pray that thou shouldest take them out of the world, but that thou shouldest keep them from the evil." Many good people think hard of themselves because they do not want to die. I have heard such persons say, "Ah me!

I am so unwilling to die, I think anyone that loves God ought to be willing to die." Well, that is against nature. It is impossible; it is wrong. The Lord Jesus Christ proposes not merely to rescue some souls from this world's ruin, but to rescue them in this world and make them live in this world as they were meant to live, by the help of his grace. This world belongs to him, and what he proposes is to take some of those—all that will come to him—that are thus oppressed by sin, and to help them here to live a life such as they should live. The idea that a person who is in health and young, with opportunities of usefulness, should want to die, is absurd. Yet many people misunderstand the matter, and think hard of themselves that they love to live and shrink from the idea of dying. When people should live a long time in the nature of things, and find nothing to live for, something is wrong about them. They may be maddened by dissatisfaction with life, or by intolerable distresses in life:

> Mad from Life's history
> Glad to Death's mystery
> Swift to be hurled;
> Anywhere, anywhere,
> Out of the world.

I read that Elijah lay under a juniper tree in the desert and requested for himself that he might die; yet really I suppose there had been no time for many years when he was not better fit to die than at that moment. In answer to his prayer, an angel came with food that he might eat and lie down and sleep again, and getting up might go work in God's service. Often when people are whining that they do not want to live, what they really need is food and sleep and exercise that they may be ready to serve God.

Now is that your desire? You feel many anxieties about life, you talk about the perils of life; is it your great struggle to escape evil, to live without sin? I do not know how it is with you, but I know how it is with Him. He ever liveth to intercede for you; and He prays that you may be kept from evil.

Then the second prayer: "Sanctify them through thy truth: thy word is truth." You observe he does not merely pray that they may be kept from evil, but that they may be made holy. Here is a common error among men about the service of Jesus Christ, the idea that it is merely a negative thing, that he proposes merely to keep them from doing evil, to keep them from doing harm. Some people think all there is in religion is to try to avoid doing harm, when Jesus goes on praying that they may be made holy. Piety is not a mere negative thing. The ten commandments, I know, are all in negative form, "thou shalt not." Even so, Christianity reveals that this is but one side, and that the other side, the nobler and more glorious side of piety, is that we must not merely try to keep from doing wrong, but try to do right. Jesus prays not simply that they may be kept from evil but that they may be made holy. My Christian hearers, I should be reluctant to ask any of you whether you think that you are holy, because those whom God would regard as holiest would be most pained to have such a question asked them. So I ask you the question, "Do you want to be holy?" and that question you should face. O men and women, you should desire to be holy! Anyhow, Jesus wishes that for you, and he prays, "Make them holy—make them holy through thy truth: thy word is truth."

It is truth that makes men holy. Earth's unholiness began with a lie that man believed and so went headlong to ruin. Truth is the lifeblood of piety. Truth is the medicine for the soul's disease. Nobody is ever made holy except through truth. Blessed be God, it often works its healing work though sadly mingled with error. The truth though it be adulterated with error, may yet through God's blessing work its healing, saving, sanctifying work. But it is only the truth that does the work. "Make them holy through thy truth." Pilate asked the question, "What is truth?" He asked the question the next morning, and here was the answer the night before, "Thy word is truth." We know that word, and we may use it as the great means of becoming holy.

Here, my brethren, I wish to offer you a practical counsel. I offer it as the result of a good deal of observation among Christian people, and of my own efforts amid a thousand infirmities and short-comings, to lead a better life. My counsel is this, regard the Bible more than you have been accustomed to do, as that which we are to use as the means of becoming holy. Regard the Bible as the great means of making you better, of making you good. Use the Bible for that purpose. I know how it is, and you will pardon me for telling you. Many times you do not love to read your Bible. The truth is, you take up your newspaper a second time and go on looking for something else in it when the Bible is lying neglected by your side. Then when you do take the Bible, you feel that it is rather dull reading. Now my counsel is, learn to regard the Bible more as the means of making you better, of making you holy. When you read it in private or hear it read in public, educate yourselves to regard it as the great means of making you better, of strengthening you, of correcting your faults, of helping you to know your duty and helping you to do your duty. Fill your heart and mind full of the teachings of God's Word, hoping it will make you better, and this course will interest you in the Bible. You will take more interest in hearing the preacher read it from the pulpit and explain and impress upon you its teachings, if you listen with the idea, "How I hope this will help me!" So in private read the Bible with the thought, "How I pray that this may do me good." Please remember this suggestion and act upon it!

Now let us consider the third petition: "That they all may be one" —"That they all may be one." Ah; I see Jesus Christ standing in that night hour with his little company of eleven. I see him sending his thoughts down the coming years to dwell upon those who through these should believe on him, and his heart went out toward them, praying "that they all may be one." I see Jesus Christ bending now from the mediator's throne with endless solicitude for every human heart that looks lovingly up to him, and knowing them all in all, the sheep of his flock on earth, and praying still "that they all may be one."

Now, my brethren, you expect me to turn round and say to you, it is not so; you expect me to contrast with this prayer the sad divisions of the Christian world. But I shall do no such thing. It is so; the prayer is answered. You say, "Very imperfectly answered"? Certainly; and so is that other prayer, "Sanctify them, make them holy," that is very imperfectly answered, and yet you would not deny that it is answered. You may deem it strange that Jesus prayed that his people might be holy, and they are so unholy, yet you do not say his prayer is not answered. In like manner or to this other prayer, Christ's true people are one, I rejoice in it and thank God. When my heart is sad at the outward divisions of the Christian world and sadder in contemplating the bitterness that so often attends these divisions, then I turn for consolation to the thought that all that truly trust in Jesus Christ, that all who love Jesus Christ in sincerity, are one. They are more one than they know, and in proportion as they are united to the Redeemer, they are united with each other. I have seen differences in families, and yet I knew they were one notwithstanding this temporary unkindness and alienation. So among Christ's children, all that are truly his, are one.

Moreover, this prayer is to be more fully answered only in the same way that the previous prayer was to be fulfilled. "Sanctify them through thy truth: thy word is truth," Yes, and "that they all may be one," through thy truth. The more gospel truth we know, and believe, and love, and live by, the more we shall be one. My friends, it seems to me that here is one of the great problems of the day in which you and I are called to live, to know how to cling to gospel truth in a spirit of broad kindliness toward those who differ from us as to what is gospel truth. Many people are so possessed with the idea that everything must be given up to the outward union of Christians that they shrink from maintaining their views as to what is gospel truth, from the notion that this would interfere with Christian union. Some have so liberalized the Christian faith that they say, "Do not blame a man for his belief; it does not make much difference what a man believes." That is, there is no assured truth; one thing is as true as another.

On the other hand, there are people who set their heads upon certain views of truth—I did not say their hearts—until there is not anything in the whole horizon of their view but those particular tenets which distinguish them from their fellow Christians. Now it is a fact that men are made better only by truth, and that Christians will be made more thoroughly one only through truth, and it is folly to sacrifice truth for the sake of union—outward union. The practical problem we have to solve is, how to maintain supreme and sovereign devotion to God's truth, and yet deal in all loving-kindness, and generous affection, and hearty co-operation, with all them that love our Lord Jesus Christ in sincerity. You say it is hard to do both of these things! Of course, it is hard to do anything well, always hard to do right and to do good, with this poor human nature of ours.

I mention one more petition. Recall those we have had. "I pray not that thou shouldest take them out of the world, but that thou shouldest keep them from the evil. Sanctify them through thy truth; thy word is truth. That they all may be one." And now finally, "Father, I will that they also, whom thou hast given me, be with me where I am; that they may behold my glory, which thou hast given me." They had beheld his humiliation, those who accompanied him, and he longed that they might be with him to behold his glory. He offers the same prayer for all that should believe on him through their word.

There are two reasons why Jesus Christ made this petition. He asked it partly for his own sake. Did you never imagine that he was sad at leaving his disciples? You know that they were sad, but was not he? Did you never suppose that he longs to have those who love him more immediately with him? He said to his disciples, Let not your heart be troubled: believe in God and believe in me, and it will all be well. I go to prepare a place for you, and if I go I will come again, and receive you unto myself. As a father taking leave of his family in going to a foreign country might say, "Now it is very sad that we are to be parted, but I am going to get a home for you, and when I get a home I will come back to you and take you there with me." He says it not only to comfort them, but more than they know perhaps, he says it to comfort his own heart also. And so Jesus said, "That they may be with me where I am." He wants to have his people with him.

But the other reason is more obvious to us; he made the prayer for their sake. He makes the prayer for our sake, "I will that they also, whom thou hast given me, be with me where I am, that they may behold my glory." To be with him is to be delivered from all the infirmities, and imperfections, and conflicts of this earthly life. I do not suppose we could bear all this if it were not for the fact that it is to end—and to end in victory. I suppose we should give over the struggling effort to do right and to do good in this world were it not for the assurance that we shall at last be conquerors and more than conquerors through him that loved us. To be with him will be to be with all who have loved us and who have gone before us to him. To be with him is to be free from all sin, and safe. Safe! O my soul, safe from all temptation to sin. To be with him is to behold his glory.

So the Saviour prays for us, and how grateful we are. Let us strive to fulfill his petitions that one day we may be with him.

LOVING JESUS CHRIST

Jesus saith to Simon Peter: Simon, son of Jonas, lovest thou me more than these? He saith unto him: Yea, Lord; thou knowest that I love thee. He saith unto him: Feed my lambs. JOHN 21:15

ALL through the summer night, the seven disciples had toiled in vain, moving their boat from one place to another, casting their net on this side and on that. However, with a fortune not uncommon in their calling, they had taken nothing at all. In the dim light of the early dawn they saw a man standing on the shore and did not know who he was. But presently he spoke to them in a kindly tone, in a familiar way, and said, "Children, have you any food?" They answered, a little grimly I suppose: "No." And he said, "Cast the net on the right side of the boat and you shall find." There was something in his tone, it may be— or something commanding in his manner—and although they had toiled so long in vain, they obeyed him. And now they were not able to draw the net into the boat for the multitude of fishes.

The character of two leading men among these disciples is here depicted as it is elsewhere in the sacred history. John, who had great sympathy with the Lord, and great spiritual insight, was the first to recognize who it was. He said, "It is the Lord." Simon Peter, as soon as this fact became known, could not wait for the rest but plunged into the sea—always impulsive and impetuous. When they came to the shore, there were fish broiling on the coals, and some bread, and they ate their humble morning meal together. It is a very homely story. It does not look as if there were much going on there, and yet the greatest things in this world, you know, have usually sprung from simple surroundings. And the best lessons of life are often to be had in lowly circumstances.

One lesson which our Lord teaches us here by his own example is, that we ought to take great pains in rebuking a friend for his fault. It is a difficult task to tell a man of his fault in such a way as to do him the most good. Many persons fail when they come roughly and blindly with their rebuke and do harm rather than good. Others see so clearly what a difficult task it is that they shrink from ever attempting it. Most of us go through life knowing that we ought to tell this person or that person about some fault or other, and we are afraid. Now our Lord has shown that he recognized it as a difficult task by the pains he has taken here to adjust all the circumstance, so that they might themselves suggest what he wanted his friend to remember for his good. Some two years before, on the shore of the same lake, there had been a like miracle when he first entered upon the service of the Lord to be a fisher of men. So the little fire around which they stood in the dimness of the early dawn clearly called to mind the incidents of a few weeks before, he had stood with others in the early morning around a little fire and the terrible thing that had happened then. When the Lord asked three times if he loved him, Peter was grieved, not merely, I suppose, because it seemed to indicate that there was room for doubt whether he really did love him, but because the three times recalled those fatal three times that he had denied his Lord. So these circumstances, carefully selected, brought it all back to his mind without the Master's needing to tell him in express words at all. Now I do think there is here a lesson for us of great importance. Let us not imagine we can perform a task with ease about which our Lord took so much pains. Let us not shrink from our duty when we see how careful he was to make all the circumstances conform to his task, with such loving consideration, with such delicate skill.

Simon Peter also gives us a lesson here, a lesson in humility to this effect. When a man is in a right mood about spiritual things he will shrink from all comparison between himself and others. Jesus said to him, "Simon, son of Jonas, lovest thou me more than these?" You know there is an ambiguity in this expression, and it exists in the Greek exactly as in the English. It may mean, more than these love, more than thou lovest these men, or more than thou lovest these pursuits. But the circumstances of the story leave no doubt as to what is meant. Peter had professed a few weeks before that he did love the Lord more than the other disciples. He had distinctly declared it, and no doubt he was sincere. When Jesus predicted that they would forsake him, Peter said, "Though all men forsake thee yet will I never forsake thee." And so he singled himself out above the other disciples, as loving the Lord more than any of them. And of that he is here reminded. But when Peter comes to answer, he leaves the comparison out this time. He says, "Lord, thou knowest that I love thee." He is in no mood for comparisons now. A truly humble man never is. He will be the last person to be thinking of such a thing, and if forced to make comparisons he will tell you that he is less than the least of all disciples, but that he does love the Lord, and the Lord does love him and he means to be a better servant.

There are many other such lessons in this narrative, but let us look immediately at the question, "Simon, son of Jonas, lovest thou me?" My friends, it has been a long time I know, long according to the centuries of human history since this question was asked. Few of us have ever stood, or ever will stand, beside the little lake of Galilee where this question was asked. Yet it is a question which lives through the ages, a question which by God's providence has come down recorded in the sacred story, a question which our loving Redeemer ever asks. It is a question which I stand humbly in his name today and desire to press home to every man, woman, and child—and I want an answer, and before God I will have an answer, from your heart of hearts. Do you love the Lord Jesus Christ? Do you love him?

But how can a man love one whom he never saw? How can he? You love many persons whom you never saw. Think of men whose books you have read and though they live far away or died long ago, still you love them dearly. Consider heroes in history, whom you have never seen, and yet you love them for their noble deeds and noble character. To be sure we can love those whom we have never seen. But another may say, "I do not hold upon this aspect of the gospel. If you talk to me about religious life; about moral living; about good deeds in the service of Jesus Christ, that seems natural for me. I see the propriety of it. If you talk about comprehending and believing the truths of the gospel, I understand that, but loving Jesus Christ, it looks to me like a sort of weak sentiment." Well, of course, religious affections will vary just as natural affections do. Men differ widely in the way in which they manifest their love to those at home. There are some persons to whom it is not natural to say much about it, and quite unnatural to deal in any tender gush of sentiment, and yet it is a thousand pities if they do not love just as truly and just as warmly as those who show it most tenderly. They show it by deeds, by an occasional kind word or look, but the love is there. And so, however differently it may be shown, we all may and we ought to and we must love Jesus Christ the Lord.

Why should we love him? Well, there are many reasons. Jesus Christ is the world's great teacher. We love our teachers, not in childhood always, for sometimes then they seem to represent to us only authority, constraint, coercion, but as we grow older there grows upon us a love of the teachers of our childhood. I went back last summer to the place where my youth was spent and saw many early friends but greatly missed a man who is still living but could not be there, a man whom I always meet with a curious love that grows on me as the years grow, the teacher of my early childhood. It is strange how one's heart does warm toward any man or woman that guided us in the times of our earliest recollection. We love our teachers, and Jesus Christ is the world's great teacher. He has taught us high and mighty motives to morality, such as were never known apart from him, even love to him, and to his Father and our Father. He has taught us our true relations to God, and the way back to God's favor. He brought life and immortality to light. How we ought to love him!

Jesus Christ is the pure example of perfect goodness. We all love goodness. Even men who are not trying to be good love goodness, even men who pretend to be worse than they are, in their hearts love goodness. But all the goodness we see besides his is mingled with imperfection, and we cannot but perceive it at times. Here is perfect goodness. Oh, how the truest sentiments of admiration ought to go out toward one, who, in human form, has been exposed to human temptations, but yielded to no temptations, and remained perfectly good. This is why we should love him!

Even though these things should bring us to love Jesus Christ, I am afraid that of themselves alone they never would. For after all they do not represent his great work in this world, his great relation to mankind. Jesus Christ is not simply the world's great teacher and the world's noblest example of purity and goodness, but far above this, Jesus Christ is a Saviour. His name Jesus meant "Jehovah saves." It was given him because he should save his people from their sins. "He came to seek and to save that which was lost." He died that men might live. "He ever liveth to intercede for them that come to God through him," that for his sake their souls may be saved. He is a Saviour. Alas! are there any here today who care nothing about salvation, who take no interest in the idea? I remember visiting the British Museum and standing one day in the Etruscan room, crowded with specimens of Etruscan and early Greek pottery, which were charming to anyone who has the least love for art or the slightest tincture of classical learnings. Presently two young men of rough appearance came to the door, and looked in, and one of them said to the other, "Tom, what would you give for all these old dishes in here?" The other replied, "Hum! I wouldn't give twopence for the whole lot." He saw no beauty in them that he should admire. You remember what the prophet said would be true concerning the great one. "We saw no beauty in him that we should admire him," that was to come, and alas! how true it is even today.

If a young man in the fullness of life and strength, and careless of everything but the pleasures of the passing moment, had come along this afternoon, driving out from the park and passed West Twenty-third Street, perhaps the last idea that would have occurred to him would be that the street is rather famous for physicians. What would he care about physicians? But let there be a sudden accident, a sudden overturning of the carriage, a limb broken, and someone coming to lift him up, then his first question would be, "Is there a good doctor close by? Can you get him quick?" So if people begin to see something of their sinfulness, and to care something for their salvation, then Jesus Christ, the Saviour of men, becomes an object of interest and love. Ah! my friends, why should we shrink from looking at that fact of our sinfulness? Is it wise for a sick man to go step by step to destruction when there is a remedy that might save him? I know it seems extravagant, but there are those here today who have had moments when they felt their whole being poisoned by sin, and their whole life blasted, who have struggled to lift themselves up above and trample down temptation until they have been despairing and humiliated and disgusted with themselves. If any such despairers will turn their looks away from themselves to Jesus Christ the Saviour of sinners and give themselves to the one task of serving him asking that they may know and do his will, leaving it to him by his grace to make them what they ought to be, then they will begin truly to love him. O soul of man, who shall give account of yourself to your God? Oh, that you would see yourself a sinful being: that you would address yourself to the Saviour and learn to love him as your Saviour and your God.

When in beginning thus to love him, we set ourselves to doing his will, every act of obedience reacts upon the love which prompts them. When, because he bids us do it, we come and go down into baptismal waters, and rise meaning for his sake to walk in newness of life, how it helps us to love him. How many here can remember the thrill of delight and the new strength with which they found themselves doing this simple thing in obedience to his command? When they gathered around the simple bread and wine and took it as a simple reminder of his dying love, doing this in remembrance of him, they have loved him more because they were acting out their love in accordance with his commandments. If that is true in ceremonies, it should be true in life, in the actual deeds of real life. Whatever we do and whatever we refrain from doing for his sake and by his help, it shall react to make us love him more.

How should we show our love to him so well as by doing good to his people? Prove your love to the Saviour by doing good to your fellow Christians. Judge them kindly, O ye Christian people, by all your own conscious weaknesses and all your stumblings, judge them kindly, and when they are weak, help them along. Doing this in love for the Lord you shall learn to love him more. That also is illustrated in the experience of ordinary life. Why, I could find you in this great city of yours a thousand examples. I could show you tomorrow evening as the day draws to its close some humble home where if you and I should go and stand and look in through the open window as the dusk came down, we should see a quiet woman approaching middle age busy with household tasks. Her cheeks are shrunken from their youthful beauty, and her complexion is faded a little. She lives in poverty and knows full well what is meant by the hard times of which we are all now speaking. But as we look in through the window she seems not sad, she seems to enjoy what she is doing. She is preparing the evening meal with toil-worn hands for the husband that is coming, and the thought of him, how it sweetens her labor—to be doing this for him, how tender it makes her heart. Presently she begins to sing and breaks off in the middle of a line, and there comes to her faded cheek a new freshness and there is a new light in her woman's eye. They used to sing that song together, when the world and they were young. Ah! love's service is pleasant service, and what we do out of love makes us love them more. This is one of the sweetest conditions of our earthly life, and it applies with all its fullness and richness to the Lord Jesus Christ. When we are doing something out of love for him we love him better. Sacrifice, self-denial, act powerfully upon the love that prompts them. That is true not only of great things but also of little things. If you stir yourself from sloth and go to the Sunday school to teach for love of the Redeemer, it will always make you love him better. If you turn away from the social gathering that is not necessary, or from some place of amusement, to go to the evening prayer meeting, it will make you love him more. If you seek out the poor and try to do them good because they are Jesus Christ's poor, you will love Jesus Christ more. If in these trying days you deny yourself gratifications though they are within your means and you would have a right to indulge in them, that you may have more to give to the thousand Christian enterprises that are struggling for existence, then your sacrifice and your self-denial will intensify your love for Christ. Whatever you do, whatever you deny yourself, out of love, it will strengthen the love that prompts it.

But let me close as the Lord himself closed the conversation. After telling Simon Peter what he must do out of love for him, he said, "Verily, verily, I say unto thee; When thou wast young, thou girdest thyself, and walkedst whither thou wouldest: but when thou shalt be old, thou shalt stretch forth thy hands, and another shall gird thee, and carry thee whither thou wouldest not." Dimly, and yet plainly, it meant that he should be crucified. And was that all that the loving Lord had to promise as a reward for a man who professed that he did love him? Thou lovest me, then serve me faithfully, and for so doing, when thou art old thou shalt be crucified. It looks strange. "This spake he, signifying by what death he should glorify God." Ah! that sheds light on it; a man that loves the Lord Jesus Christ is a man that means to live so as to glorify God. He promised Simon Peter a death of suffering and outward shame, but in that death he should glorify God.

My brethren, we live in a world of failures. How many businessmen in this city fail sometime or other. We live in a time of failures. Everything in this world is in danger of failing except one thing: a man who is really living to glorify God—that man will not fail, that end will be accomplished. It may not be in the way you had fancied or preferred, but in the way which he sees to be more for your good and more for his glory. You wanted to glorify him in a long life crowded with useful deeds; he may appoint that you shall glorify him by an early death. You wanted to glorify him with ample means, which you would scatter far abroad with holy love; he may want you to bear poverty with dignity. You thought you would glorify him in a life of health and strength, doing good in the world; and he may have thought to try you amid the sufferings of a sickbed. It is not for a laborer in the vineyard to choose himself where he will work, but only to work where he is placed. We know not what awaits us, but if in simplicity and godly sincerity, in such calling and circumstances as providence assigns us, we do make it our aim to glorify God, then whatever crashes and falls around us, life will not be failure, but will show our love and glorify our Saviour!

13

IN JESUS' NAME

Verily, verily, I say unto you, whatsoever ye shall ask the Father in my name, he will give it you. Hitherto have ye asked nothing in my name: ask, and ye shall receive, that your joy may be full. JOHN 16:23, 24

THE text is a part of our Saviour's last discourse to his disciples. In order to understand it one should read Chapters 14, 15, and 16 of John.

These words present four topics of reflection on prayer in Christ's name.

I. Up to this time men had not asked in Christ's name. "Hitherto have ye asked nothing in my name." Our Saviour's mediatorical character had not been fully understood and recognized. Disciples had come to him with requests, and some of them were requests which only the divine Being could grant, such as "Increase our faith." It was difficult, perhaps impossible, for them fully to understand the Saviour's relation to prayer and to salvation, while he was yet with them. It was difficult for them to realize his divinity, to think of him as being everywhere present. Moreover, the especial ground of his mediatorship was his atoning death, and this they never understood till after it occurred. While Christ's mediatorship, which is always the ground on which prayer is really heard, was not yet recognized, now they were taught to "ask the father in My name."

II. What is implied in asking in Christ's name?

1. It implies acknowledgment of personal unworthiness. It says that a man does not expect to be heard in his own name. Men who reject doctrine of mediation often say that they are magnifying God's mercy; but is it not magnifying man's merit? Here lies the greatest cause of dislike to the doctrine of atonement. You find such men always cherish high opinion of human excellence.

It is this conceit of personal merit, actual or attainable, that keeps men away from reliance on Christ. Self-reliance, it cannot too often be urged, is the great obstacle to salvation. Now to ask in the name of Christ is to cast this away, to acknowledge personal unworthiness.

2. It implies acquiescence in the divine provision for our acceptance. This cannot be said to require any particular degree of acquiescence with the nature of this provision. Many who just recognize the bare fact that we are heard for Jesus' sake and not for our own, this they accept upon declaration of God's Word. But Scriptures do teach much concerning its nature. Christ the mediator is both God and man —and therefore appropriate that through him man should draw near to God. But to consider more narrowly, take the saying of John, "Adversary with the Father." Observe that the man conscious of sin, thinks of his Adversary as righteous—and more, as the propitiation for our sins. Again, take the view presented in Hebrews, to my mind the clearest and most attractive in the Scriptures. We have a great High Priest, Jesus the Son of God—he has passed into the heavens, has offered in the true sanctuary the everlasting sacrifice, which needs not to be repeated, and so he is able to save those who come unto God by him. But not only is he able to save; he has compassion on us, "touched with a feeling of our infirmities," etc. Now notice the apostle's conclusion from these two great facts, that we have a High Priest who is able to save and desires to save—"Let us therefore come boldly to the throne of grace," etc. Observe, it is the throne of grace, and we have come to obtain mercy, yet we come with confidence because we have such a mediator.

This precious promise is sometimes misunderstood or caricatured, as if the Supreme Sovereign were vindictive, disposed to treat men harshly, and only brought into a different mind by the pleadings of his Son. Observe verses 26 and 27. All that believe in Christ, that ask in his name, are loved of the Father. And more—it was God's love that led to this provision. "Herein is love, not that we loved God, but that he loved us, and sent his Son to be the propitiation for our sins." And thus he "commendeth his love to us." At the same time, he is angry with the wicked, and must punish, while pitying and desiring that they might turn and live. There is a difference between love of complacency and a love of compassion.

III. Encouragement to ask in Christ's name. "Whatsoever ye shall ask," etc.

Of course, this must be taken with certain limitations. This is true of many general statements of Scripture; we need not be surprised at this, for the same thing is constantly done in all use of human language. However, we are not left to our own judgment concerning the limitations. We are taught by the same inspired apostle who recorded the text. "If we ask anything according to his [e.g., Christ's] will," I John 5:14, 15. Now we know that some things we may ask, may not be always God's will to bestow, such as temporal blessings. But spiritual blessings are always asked according to his will. Do we ask conversion? "He is not willing that any should perish." Do we ask progress in piety? "This is the will of God, even your sanctification." Final salvation? "Even so it is not the will of our Father which is in heaven, that one of these little ones [viz., those who believe in him] should perish" (Matt. 18:14).

Then be encouraged to ask in Christ's name. My hearers, why do you not all pray? Are you ashamed to pray? Are you afraid to pray? A man may well be afraid, but there is the mediator—ask in his name. Is there nothing you need, which can be obtained only by prayer? Then pray!

IV. The result of asking in Christ's name. "That your joy may be full."

Here is a promise of joy-full joy, even though the disciples were sorrowful. All through this discourse, he was directing their thoughts to the future, declaring that their sorrow should be turned into joy. How fully this came to pass, even by the very event which now caused them bitter sorrow. It became the especial source of joy to them and to all mankind. This is a peculiar case—yet often God causes gladness to spring up from the midst of grief. To many affliction has proved to be a blessing, often leading to conversion or new consecration. The gay shrink from religion, imagining that all joy would be gone; the pious cling to religion, knowing that it can gild the clouds of life's inevitable sorrows with a heavensent joy. Yes, piety brings joy.

But more narrowly, "Ask, etc. that your joy may be full." What is the relation of prayer to joy? We might say that the very fact of communion with God is joy. Confidence of acceptance through the mediator is a source of delight.

But it is by the answer to our prayers that our joy may be full. (1) Ask for clearer practical views of justification by faith. Lack of this produces the gloom of many Christians. Ask those who have been brought out of such seasons into joy and peace. (2) Ask for sanctifying influences of God's Spirit, that you may be drawn near to God and kept near, filled with all the fullness of those blessings which God bestows. "Keep yourselves in the love of God, praying in the Holy Ghost."

Ask most of all things for these, and your joy may be full. Whatever be your lot, you shall have joy in believing. Brethren, it is clear that we "have not, because we ask not"? "Ask etc. that your joy may be full." And though from weak faith and feeble petitions we should come short of joy complete on earth, yet . . . "in thy presence is fullness of joy," etc.

Behold the high privileges of the Christian to ask in the name of Christ and to know this joy.

14

DELIGHT IN THE WILL OF GOD

I delight to do thy will, O my God! PSALM 40:8

THIS psalm tells of one who has suffered, been graciously relieved, and now responds in grateful praise and grateful obedience. This is not shown by mere externals of worship, but by delighting to do God's will, by having his law in the heart, by proclaiming his glorious character and gracious dealings (verses 1–10).

Verses 5–9 apply to Christ. So it is with various psalms; often the language is exclusively prophetic of him. These words, therefore, are designed to be adopted by anyone, while at the same time it may look to the great example of the Lord Jesus Christ. Observe, that this delight is not merely to hear, but to do, the will of God.

I. In one sense, the will of God will always be done, whether we do his will or not.

Here we touch a most difficult subject but we need not turn away from it; but we must be humble, and content to take what we can understand, and leave alone what we cannot.

We are compelled to speak of God's will in terms applicable to our own. This is done in Scripture. There are three distinct senses in which this term is employed. First, the will of purpose; it is always done. "Who worketh all things after the counsel of his own will"—"Who doeth his will in the army of heaven, and among," etc. (Dan. 5:35). Next, the will of desire, or wish, which is not always done—for inscrutable reasons he permits free agents to act counter to his wish —"How often would I, etc. but ye would not." "Not willing that any should perish," etc. "Who willeth all to be saved," etc. Last, will of command—the wish of one in authority, when expressed, becomes a command. Every command of God it is our solemn duty to obey— but, alas! It is not always done. Of course, it is human imperfection that makes these distinctions necessary, and they must not be pushed too far—yet they are, within limits, just distinctions, and should be borne in mind.

115

Now God's purpose, as distinguished from other senses, is not dependent upon us for accomplishment. It may be accomplished without us, by overruling and finding others willing. But God's will of desire, what is well-pleasing to him, we should seek to ascertain, and do. His will of command we should learn and obey.

How do we ascertain what is God's will? Partly from our own conscience, aided by general conscience of mankind, but this is by no means an infallible exponent of God's will. What has come to pass, is always in accordance with God's general purpose, however wrong the motives of agents—gives indication as to what we should do. To some extent we may seek the best judgment and advice of others. It is always important to have the mind stored with Scripture. Then we can pray and trust we are doing God's will.

II. We should always do God's will, even if it be not with delight.

We seldom, if ever, do anything with perfectly correct motives and feelings. Yet with the most proper sentiments we can at the time command, let us still do our duty.

Sometimes we cannot rise above resignation. Especially when we have to bear what disappoints and distresses us.

Sometimes we may do his will with shrinking and reluctance. Human nature is weak. Even apart from sin, it naturally shrinks from danger, suffering, physical or mental. Even Jesus, to whom the text specially applied. "And now what shall I say? Father, save me from this hour? But," etc. Again, "If it be possible, etc. nevertheless, not my will, but thine be done." This cost an effort, and a struggle, for a time—yet he did not fail to do it.

Yes, we should always do God's will, even if it is not a delight. And often, the painful effort will change to pleasure, the duty commenced reluctantly will become a sweet joy!

Yet, do not condition obedience upon its becoming delightful. It is the will of my God? Then his will I must do.

III. We should delight to do God's will.

We may be led to it.

1. By sense of right. The vexing question of ethical speculation does not here matter—whether God wills a thing because right, or it is right because he wills it. What he wills, is right. To do right is man's highest duty, and should be his greatest delight.

2. By feelings of interest. It is right to consult our own improvement and enjoyment. Lawful to be pleased at advancing these, provided we are doing God's will. Now always our true interest, in noblest sense, on largest scale, to do God's will. Hence self-love should conspire with a sense of right in causing us to delight in God's will.

3. By feelings of benevolence. I hope no one present is wholly ignorant of the pleasure derived from benefiting others. "And learn the luxury of doing good" (Goldsmith). Now in doing God's will, we may be sure we are promoting the well-being of our fellow men—whether we can always perceive the connection or not. If it is God's will, it shall be best for all we love, for all mankind, that this should be done. What a pleasure, then, it should be, to do his will.

4. By feelings of gratitude. My brethren, let us think of all our providential and spiritual blessings. And while our hearts glow with gratitude, for all God has done, and is doing, and promises to do for us, shall we not be able to say, "I delight to do thy will, O my God!"

In doing God's will, we follow the example of Jesus—seen in his whole life, and declared in his own words. (John 4:34) Remember him at Jacob's well—fatigued, needing rest and food, yet busy doing good, and yet saying to his disciples, "My meat is to do the will of him that sent me, and to finish his work." In doing this, we are dear to Jesus. (Matt. 12:46–50) "Whosoever shall do the will of my Father which is in heaven, the same is my brother, and sister, and mother." We become as near as the dearest kindred.

Oh, it is sweet to do God's will. Oh, ye who delight to do his will, go on, and it shall grow more and more delightful—go on, and the path you tread shall grow more and more a path of light, till it shall lead you into the dazzling glories of the celestial world; and there, oh there, in perfect obedience you shall find perfect delight.

And meanwhile, however, the number shall be multiplying on earth, of those who delight to do God's will. The prayer our Saviour taught his disciples to pray shall rise from many a pious heart, shall stimulate many a toiling brain, shall nerve many a weary laborer, in Christian and in heathen lands, till Christianity, everywhere triumphant, shall cover the earth in a flood of glory, till God's will shall be done on earth, as it is done in heaven.

LESSONS FOR THE TEMPTED

Wherefore let him that thinketh he standeth, take heed lest he fall. There hath no temptation taken you but such as is common to man: but God is faithful, who will not suffer you to be tempted above that ye are able; but will with the temptation also make a way to escape, that ye may be able to bear it. I CORINTHIANS 10:12, 13

HERE is a text which speaks to our need. Though temptation comes, we do not understand it and are often not prepared for it. Through Paul, God is giving us guidance to help us. There are four points suggested by the text as regards temptation.

I. We recognize here that God suffers us to be tempted. "God is faithful; he will not suffer you to be tempted above that you are able." Then God suffers us to be tempted. This is a distinction which does not amount to a great deal, I confess, and yet which is useful and helps us somewhat in relieving the dark mystery of evil in this world, that God permits evils of which he is not the author. We shrink back with horror from the idea of regarding him as the author of evil, we cannot believe it; and it helps us a little to think that God permits evils of which he is not the author. He suffers us to be tempted. The apostle James says that God tempts no man. "Let no man say when he is tempted, I am tempted of God: for God cannot be tempted with evil, neither tempteth he any man." The word "tempt," as you all know—and the same thing is true of the words in the original language—signifies "to test," "to put to the test"—as when you test a gun. This testing may be done with a good or an evil design. A man may put a great charge of powder into a gun for the purpose of ascertaining whether it is strong and can stand the test! or he may do it for the purpose of ascertaining whether it is weak, for the purpose of destroying it. So human character may be tested with friendly feelings, to try its strength, or with hostile feelings, in order to show its weakness and to destroy it. In the bad sense of the term God tempts nobody, but he suffers us to be tempted.

Shall we inquire why he does this? We might say that temptation is one of the conditions of existence in this world. We cannot see how it would be possible to live here without being tempted. Jesus Christ himself, who was sinless, who came into this world to live but a little while and to die, endured temptation, not once merely, but many times—tempted to do what was wrong in the desert, tempted in the garden to shrink from what he had undertaken to do. Temptation is a condition of our existence.

Moreover, temptation is a discipline. That is one of the reasons why we may say God permits us to be tempted. Here again we have the example of Jesus. We are told in the Epistle to the Hebrews that Jesus learned from what he suffered. His human nature needed discipline like ours, and it found discipline in temptation as we do. He learned from what he suffered, and thus being made perfect he became the author of eternal salvation. So much for the first point: God suffers us to be tempted.

II. Now the second point: We should be afraid of temptation. "Let him that thinketh he standeth, take heed lest he fall." There are two forms of peril against which we need to caution ourselves. It is a perilous thing to question the reality and the power of temptation. Why, my friends, if there be such a being as Satan, if he has such designs against us and against God as the Scriptures plainly declare, then what could please him better than that men should deny his existence? What could help him more?

But I said there were two forms of peril. If it is perilous that we should be heedless about temptation, its reality and its power, it is peculiarly perilous that we should feel a self-confident presumption that we can overcome it. "Let him that thinketh he standeth, take heed lest he fall." Ah! a man who is afraid he will fall may, perhaps, take care, but a man who thinks he stands will seldom take heed.

III. The third point in the text is, that we must not excuse ourselves when we are tempted. We must not excuse ourselves with the idea that it is impossible to resist temptation. We must not imagine that we have nothing to do with it and that temptation comes as a power from without and presses in upon us, and we are helpless. Temptation becomes temptation to us only as something within us rises up to meet the allurement from without. James tells us: "Every man is tempted, when he is drawn away by his own desire, and enticed." He is seduced by his own soul's desire, and only his own soul's desire can really lead him to sin. The power from without may be mighty, and yet the man is a free man and yields to temptation only when something within him goes forth to meet that which comes from without. Yet how common a thing it is to imagine we cannot help yielding to temptation. It is not impossible to resist temptation. At any rate when we do not resist, it is our fault. If we really have not now the power to resist, this may be only a punishment for having failed to resist in other days when we might have done it.

Again, we must not excuse ourselves as we are so often inclined to do, with the idea that our temptations are very peculiar. "There hath no temptation taken you," says the apostle, "but such as is common to man." Yet how very general is the notion that our trials and our temptations are certainly the most peculiar and the hardest to bear that any poor, wretched human being has ever had to face. It seems to be a universal human tendency. You cannot help thinking that people whose character is very different from yours, whose surroundings are different, do not have strong temptations. Of course, particular forms of temptation are mightier to one person and less mighty to another. But take the sum total, and if we saw things as the high angels see them, if we saw things as God sees them, we should never delude ourselves with that dream.

IV. Now, finally, trusting in God we can conquer temptation. For God will help us, the text implies, both by his providence and by his grace. "God is faithful, who will not suffer you to be tempted above that ye are able; but will with the temptation also make the way of escape, that ye may be able to bear it." My friends, God has often done that for us already. If you have advanced far enough in life to see the meaning of your past life, can you not look back and see how, when God's providence brought you into temptation, there has also been provided the way of escape? That is what the text implies that he will do for us if we trust in him, the faithful God. If enlightened by his Word and if seeking his grace to guide us, though we meet with temptation, there will be somewhere, somehow, a door opened that we may escape. Oh, blessed be God that he is controlling all these mighty forces of evil which move around us, so that the temptations themselves sometimes counteract one another. The more we are tempted the more we are safe sometimes. Ah! when we are sorely tempted, God will not fail to open the way of escape, if we have a heart to seek for it, a soul that longs to find it.

Not only by his providence, but by his grace, God will help us in our temptation. If strengthened by God's grace, if filled with a hatred, a mortal hatred of sin, we struggle against it, then we shall trample temptation under foot. We shall know the discipline of character which comes from temptation conquered. "Happy is the man," says the apostle James "that endureth temptation: for when he has stood the test, he shall receive the crown of life, which the Lord hath promised to them that love him." Therefore, he said, "My brethren, count it all joy when ye fall into divers temptations." If we trust God's providential help and his gracious Spirit, then we can see how temptation may be the means of making us better; and, rising up in grateful joy and trust, we may rejoice with James, "Knowing that the testing of our faith worketh patience. But let patience have a perfect work, that we may be perfect and entire, lacking in nothing. If any man lack wisdom—wisdom to take these wholesome views of temptation, wisdom to find the way out of temptation, wisdom to see the meanings of temptation and gain its lessons—if any man lack wisdom, let him ask of God, who giveth to all men liberally, and upbraideth not; and it shall be given him."

My brethren, I ask not today for you and that we may have a life without trial and temptation. I should be afraid to ask it; for "whom the Lord loveth, he chasteneth"; and it is the law of earthly existence that we shall be tempted. But I humbly ask for myself and for you that we may have grace to help us watch and strive against temptation, grace to trample it under foot, grace to conquer it.

16

THE GOOD SHEPHERD

I am the good shepherd. JOHN 10:11

PASTORAL life, always more common in East than West, early became associated in men's minds and in literature with ideas of peace and tranquil enjoyment. Likewise, pastoral life has yielded many beautiful images to the inspired writers. But they used figures to teach spiritual truths. Many of the most famous men connected with the history of Israel were themselves shepherds.

Isaiah, looking forward to the Messiah, amid the more splendid imagery with which he represents him, touches our tenderest feeling when saying (40:11), "He shall feed his flock," etc.

So when Jesus came, he frequently availed himself of this same image. He does not scrupulously adhere to the figure of a shepherd, nor need we. Consider him.

I. As giving his life for the sheep.

1. He came, not as the thief [false teachers], but that they might have life. John 10:10.

Imagine a flock, scattered, panic-struck because a furious lion has assailed them. But the shepherd comes and soon lies dead in their defense; but the lion lies dead beside him, and the flock is safe. Heroic man, how he would be honored among the rustic people—his remains, his name. You see the parallel—so may angels honor our shepherd. But here the parallel ends—he died, yet he lives, to move among those he has died to save, to be loved and followed with new affection. He laid down his life that he might take it again.

2. He died voluntarily, John 10:15, 18.

(a) Disciples were likely to think, when so often told in advance, and when his hour came, that men were compelling his death. In one sense this is true, in another it is purely voluntary. They could not, except he had chosen.

(b) The Father did not compel him to do it. Objection is sometimes made to atonement here—yet innocent not forced to suffer for guilty, it was voluntary.

(c) But was it right that he should suffer, even voluntarily? He felt he had the right. See John 10:18.

We could never have asked him to die for us. If it were now to be decided, that he should be humiliated, suffer, die, to save us from destruction, every just and generous feeling would prompt us to say, "No. Let me bear what I have merited—let him not suffer for me." Nonetheless, without our knowledge he did suffer and suffered out of love. Shall we reject him? Now it is no longer a question, "Shall he die for us?" He did! "In his love and in his pity he redeemed us." Shall we accept the benefits secured by his dying love—shall we be grateful—love him—be his? Consider

II. His tender care of his flock.

1. He knows them by name, John 10:14. No danger that in the multitude anyone will be overlooked or forgotten. He knows every individual, and intimately.

2. He pursues the straying—"goeth into the mountains." This applied primarily to his coming into our world to seek and save the lost. Same thing is true of his gracious dealing with wanderers from his fold, backsliders. Such wanderers should return to the shepherd and bishop of our souls.

3. He deals gently with recent and feeble believers. Passage in Isa. 40:11—"he shall gather the lambs with his arm, and bear them in his bosom." This does not refer to children particularly, as context would place beyond question, but to those who have recently become believers, and are feeble. He will take care, shelter, bear along, strengthen. May your faith "grow exceedingly." Now babes in Christ, you shall become perfect (full-grown) men in Christ Jesus.

4. He supports in danger and difficulty.

The shadow of death is a highly poetical expression for the profoundest darkness. Conceive a flock led by the shepherd through a valley, deep, overshadowed, dark, where savage wild beasts abound, and yet they are fearless because the shepherd is with them. So we in seasons when, figuratively, our path lies through a dark valley, we will not fear because the Shepherd will be present. In affliction, when apt to feel deserted and desolate, he will be near, will uphold and comfort. How beautiful, how delightful to a flock which has been passing through a dark valley, will be the green pastures and quiet waters. And often when you have been afflicted, the subsequent seasons of health, prosperity, tranquil happiness, have been more delightful by reason of the shivering terror with which you had passed through that dark valley.

5. He guards in temptation. The flock, in a deep and dark valley, is especially exposed to wild beasts. So we have dreadful foes—"our adversary, the devil, as a roaring lion, walketh about, seeking whom he may devour" (I Pet. 5:8). The apostle here referred especially to persecution. The great enemy commonly comes against us. The Scripture has an expression more beautiful, and not less impressive— "Satan transformed into an angel of light" (II Cor. 11:14). Temptation has a dreadful power.

> In the way a thousand snares
> Lie to take us unawares;
> Satan, with malicious art,
> Watches each unguarded part;
> But from Satan's malice free,
> Saints shall soon victorious be;
> Soon the joyful news will come,
> "Child, your Father calls; come home."

6. He will continue to preserve them to the end, John 10:27–29. This great truth is repeatedly and strongly taught in Scripture. If we become really his, he will not forsake us, we shall never cease to be his. The ground of this is in his power and unchangeableness—assurance of it is in his promises.

Some are afraid to undertake a life of piety, lest they should not hold out. Will the Saviour hold out? He will give unto us eternal life —we shall never perish.

Now how should the flock feel and act toward such a shepherd? Only time for these things:

(a) Confide in his protecting care.

(b) Cherish toward him a tender affection. The love of the flock for their shepherd here a rebuke and a stimulation to us.

(c) Follow him with unhesitating obedience.

17

THE LIGHT OF LIFE

In him was life: and the life was the light of men. And the light shineth in darkness; and the darkness comprehended it not. JOHN 1:4, 5

EVERY attentive reader must have been struck with the introduction to the Gospel of John. It is calculated and designed to give more correct and exalted conceptions of the dignity of him who became our Redeemer—that we may recognize his claims upon our love and obedience. Who can fail to take interest in the inspired account of such a subject! From the very nature of the subject, the passage contains much that is difficult—but without going beyond our depth, without wild and vain speculation, we may find our profit in dwelling upon the various parts of this introduction, which will come up in the process of explaining and commenting upon the verses read.

I. In *him*. Whom? The Word. Consider

1. The allusions to his pre-existence and divinity. We may suppose (with reverence) that sacred writers often had great difficulty in finding suitable terms—never more than here. The term "Word" (*logos*) had come to be much used to denote an exalted being, supposed to have a very intimate relation to the Deity. Later Jewish writers identify or at least connect this *logos* with the word of God —especially Philo, who is said to have employed the term frequently, and to have referred to a peculiar use of it made by Plato. In the speculations which were already becoming rife in Asia Minor, the term was largely employed to express various ideas of a divine being which were absurd and even blasphemous. Now the apostle adopted the term as coming nearest, not sanctioning these erroneous notions, but making such statements as were calculated to correct them—setting forth the real and true Word, in opposition to all false and fantastical notions.

(a) This exalted Being existed in the beginning.

(b) He was with God—intimate communion, enjoyment of glory and blessedness.

(c) He was God. Plain, explicit, unambiguous. Numerous other statements like it.

(d) Repeated statement that he was with God, seems to refer to the distinction of persons—the Word was God, and the Word was with God. How much the Scriptures explicitly declare concerning the divinity of the Father, the Son, and the Holy Spirit, and yet that God is one. Terms "person" and "Trinity" are of human choosing, but the best perhaps that we can find.

(e) He was the Creator of all things.

2. His incarnation—"The Word was made flesh, and dwelt among us, full of grace and truth—and we beheld his glory," etc. A real incarnation—"forasmuch as the children were partakers of flesh and blood, he also" etc.

II. "In him was life." Various terms employed in this introduction, which require and would repay a careful study, comparing especially the apostle's own use of them elsewhere. Besides Word, we have *life, light, darkness, grace* and *truth,* the *world,* etc.

Life—Cf. John 5:26. "As the Father hath life in himself, even so," etc. I John 1:1, 2.—"Of the Word of Life; for the Life was manifested, and we have seen it, and bear witness, and shew unto you that eternal life which was with the Father, and was manifested unto us." Thus he is represented as the self-subsisting source of Life, the fountain of life.

Again, as appointed to impart spiritual life. John 14:6. "I am the way, and the truth, and the life." I John 5:11. God hath given to us eternal life, and this life is in his Son. In him is life then, in the most extensive sense.

III. "And the life was the *light* of *men.*" The vitalizing, fructifying principle. Light used in Scripture is expressive of knowledge and happiness.

1. Knowledge. As sight is the chief means of gaining knowledge of external world, so very naturally light is the emblem of knowledge in general. He has given knowledge.

(a) Of immortality. So much more certainly and distinctly known.

(b) Of the attributes of God, and our relations to him.

(c) Of the way in which guilty man may be justified and saved. Notice this especially.

2. Happiness. What a world of darkness is ours—not simply mental, but spiritual darkness! He the Sun of Righteousness. Think of the happiness derivable from knowledge of the coming life. Still

more happiness comes from knowledge and personal experience of the way of salvation.

The true Light, which coming into the world, lighteth every man. Not Jews alone, but "a light to lighten the Gentiles"—his mission is not restricted in its design, whatever may be true of its actual application.

IV. "And the light shineth in darkness, and the darkness comprehended it not." (Received it not.) Men are in the spiritual ignorance and misery which belong to sin.

1. These received not the light. The world, made by him, yet knew him not. His own received him not. Often they who seem specially favored, do most utterly reject the Saviour. They loved darkness rather than light, because their deeds were evil.

2. We may rejoice that the statement could not be made without exception—there have always been some to receive him. To them he gave the right, privilege, to become the sons of God—to as many as received him, and not Jews alone. And these were not such by virtue of any natural birth, but by spiritual birth—born of God. Cf. "born of water and of the Spirit," the pure birth of the Spirit.

And now, my friends, do not wonder that I have failed to give any very clear and complete conceptions of these great truths; these are things the angels desire to look into—they shall be our study through eternity. Who can grasp the vast ideas here shadowed forth—who comprehend the mystery of the Trinity, the Incarnation—or appreciate all that is meant here by life, by darkness and light? A full comprehension and appreciation is reserved for the coming state. But we know enough for all the ends of life, all the wants of our spiritual being, if we will receive the light, and act upon it. To which class shall we belong, those who receive, or those who reject, the Light of the World, the only Saviour?

18

THE PRAYER OF THE WOMAN OF CANAAN

MATTHEW 15:21–28

NEVER, save on this occasion, did our Lord go beyond the border of Palestine. He was a "minister of the circumcision"—"not sent but unto the lost sheep of the house of Israel." He did not absolutely restrict his benefits to the Jews, for centurions as well as this woman knew his healing power. But the Gentile restriction, and the hesitation here, may seem strange in view of the fact that the peculiar glory of the gospel was that its benefits should extend to the Gentiles, that the exclusiveness of the Jewish system was to be broken down. It seems to be a part of that obvious plan in God's moral government that great changes are not made suddenly, but gradually, as man was to be prepared to receive. The Messiah was the son of David—his dispensation was to be an enlargement and consummation of the Jewish system, and so the foundations of his kingdom must be laid in Israel.

Now the best of the Jews could not be prepared at once for fraternizing with the Gentiles; therefore, had Jesus gone out among the Gentiles in the beginning, and placed them on the same footing, he would have shocked prejudices so as to gain no Jewish disciples. Even after his ascension, it required providential scattering and special vision to convince Peter that this was proper. Accordingly, he confined himself to his own nation and so did the seventy. But when his own work was finished, when the Holy Spirit came with his teachings, when the great principles of the Messiah's reign were more fully understood, then the apostles went preaching "repentance and remission of sins unto all nations."

But as Jesus went into the coasts of Tyre and Sidon, he met a woman whose daughter was "grievously vexed with the devil." This woman's concern for her daughter expressed itself in a prayer which deserves our study and imitation in both its matter and its spirit. Let us notice them.

I. The subject of her prayer.

She prayed for blessings on her child. Many of us would pray thus too, if a child were so posesssed. Some who neglect religion have at such a time made agonized petitions to God and made promises to him.

But are not your children and those of your friends diseased? Are they not, in a most important sense, affected with the disease of sin and under the power of Satan. I do not doubt you pray for them, often and earnestly, much more than they suppose. Sometimes you long to speak to them, yet you are afraid to do so. Therefore, you go away and pour it out before the Lord.

But do you pray as you should? With such earnestness as this woman manifested? Making each case your own? Christian parent, think often of your son, your daughter, living as they do. Pray for them; live rightly before them; and seek in every way to win them to Christ. It will be better for you, though not lessening their guilt, if they die before you, or are left behind you, impenitent; it will be a comfort if you can ere long be joined with them in Christian hope, and when you depart to be with Christ, can know that they are pressing toward the mark. In view of death, and eternity, pray, Christian hearers, for your dear kindred, and for your children.

II. The character of her prayer.

1. It was a believing prayer.

She believed that Jesus was Messiah, the "Son of David," and that he was able and willing to heal her child. How great was her faith! Has he not the power and willingness to save us, to bless us with spiritual blessings?

2. It was an humble prayer.

She was willing to take the position Jesus gave her. So should it be with us. We should stand where God's Word places us. But many are not willing to do this. When God's Word declares them depraved, they defend themselves against the charge. When God's Word calls them guilty, they deny or seek to extenuate. When God offers them salvation as a free gift, they are unwilling to accept. This, for the unconverted, is a matter of great importance, to stand where God places you, and accept what God offers you.

Many beautiful instances of humility might be found in Scripture, such as the centurion, publican, and Paul, but none is more worthy of imitation than the humble plea of the woman of Phoenicia.

3. It was persevering prayer.

The object of our Lord's seeming repulse was probably to test the perseverance of her faith. She persevered because she really desired what she sought. Her perseverance won her desire.

Here is a prayer which is worthy of imitation. Here is a spirit which we could well imitate.

19

THE PLEASURES OF PIETY

Her ways are ways of pleasantness,
And all her paths are peace. PROVERBS 3:17

SOME have thought it wrong that Christianity should appeal so much
to the desire of happiness—most men, on the contrary, dislike its re-
quirement of self-denial. As objections, a French preacher has well
said, we might leave them to refute each other. But then both statements are true—and religion herein corresponds with human nature
as we find it. Men in general have a conflict between feeling of interest and of duty—desiring gratification, yet feeling that they ought to
deny themselves. Religion proposes to reunite and harmonize these
so that the desire for happiness may be satisfied with holiness; that
not only interest in fact, but men's *feeling* of interest, may coincide
with duty—and while denying themselves all unlawful gratification,
they may have new desires, whose gratification shall afford real
happiness. Religion should make us happy, for love is the fulfilling
of the law, and love is happiness. Religion may properly appeal to
our desire for happiness, because we cannot exercise love to others
without self-love. Selfishness, the perversion, the caricature of this,
is wrong, but self-love is a necessary part of our nature, indispensable to our loving others, and thus indispensable to religion.

Condescending to our infirmities, and seeing that men have lost
the relish for holiness, God appeals to their relish for happiness. If
attracted by this, they may then be less averse to holiness. But observe, there is no compromise—it is not by the offer of sensual
pleasures, here or hereafter, that we would attract men to religion.
We do not say that you can be religious, and still enjoy the pleasures
of sin. We do insist that you can be religious, and still have pleasure.
It would not do if happiness were the sole object in seeking religion—
but it may attract, and other elements enter in afterward.

Take this, then, as the subject of the sermon, "Religion affords
Happiness," or, "The Pleasures of Piety."

I. The influence of piety upon those objects and relations which are commonly thought to contribute most to happiness.

1. Influence upon length of days. How religion contributes to this. Even conscientious care, even strong religious principle, fails to save many persons from neglect of health; but what would become of them without such principles?

2. Influence upon reputation. Consistent piety secures respect and confidence. Those who are religious should refuse to compromise with others. They may be annoyed, even vexed, at your refusal, yet in their hearts they will honor you. A firm, decided stand is easiest to maintain, and at the same time most reputable.

3. Influence on riches. I cannot speak of this, any more than the former topics, at length. Riches do not of themselves make a man pious—they often, though not always, have a contrary effect. Piety does not necessarily promote wealth—but it must always have that tendency. It deters from vices, and vice is commonly expensive. It enjoins and encourages those virtues, which are promotive of wealth, as frugality.

4. Influence upon our social relations. Affection for kindred and friends is enhanced by piety and mutual duties are performed better where there is piety. Piety gives a greater disposition to forgiveness and to self-sacrifice. It sheds a new luster over the brightest home, bestows an added joy upon the most loving hearts.

With reference to all these, observe the disposition religion produces, as regards both prosperity and adversity. Piety gives contentment, the disposition to make the best of everything. How great the value of this to happiness!

II. The new sources of happiness which piety opens up within us. Piety opens up many new sources of happiness.

1. Trust in providence. Rather than "trusting to luck," or trusting merely to the uniformity of the laws of nature, we place our trust in a personal God who governs all things by his powerful Word. How immense the importance to our happiness of regarding the doings of providence as the work of our Father.

2. Peace of spirit. This grows out of reconciliation with God. How often the happiness of the impenitent is marred by thoughts of his danger as the enemy of God.

But reconciliation with God, what a ground for peace of spirit—appropriating all the gracious promises, resting upon them, delighting in them.

Then we may be able, by God's grace helping, to attain peace of conscience.

3. The enjoyment of religious exercises. Piety makes our worship, both public and private, pleasant.

In seasons of private prayer and in Scripture reading, truth comes with unwonted clearness and preciousness.

4. Self-sacrifice for the good of others.

5. The hope of eternal blessedness.

Let it not be objected then to religion, that it would destroy happiness. It confers the highest happiness in life, the only happiness in death and in eternity.

20

SIN AND FORGIVENESS

> If we say that we have no sin, we deceive ourselves, and the truth is not in us. If we confess our sins, he is faithful and just to forgive us our sins, and to cleanse us from all unrighteousness. If we say that we have not sinned, we make him a liar, and his word is not in us. I JOHN 1:8–10

THE apostle is making an earnest, vehement protest against living in sin, when one professes to be Christian. God is Light, and in him no darkness at all—to say therefore that we have fellowship with him, and walk in darkness is to lie.

But here must arise in the mind of even the earnest Christian the thought that he has sinned, even though with all his efforts he has striven to walk only in the light, yet he has sinned. The apostle regards this state of mind and calls attention to the provision for pardon of our sins. In the midst of such arguments and precepts occurs the text.

Suppose one stood up before an audience such as this to speak of innocence and excellence and merited felicitation. How utopian! You would call him a fool or a maniac. But I come but to speak of sin and salvation. Hear then for your soul's salvation, hear for eternity.

I. The evils of denying that we are sinners.

1. To do this is to deceive ourselves.

(a) Some foolishly make professions of sinless perfection.

(b) Unconverted men are often unwilling to face self-examination and delude themselves.

(c) It is a delusion. God's Word, here and elsewhere, declares we are sinners. Our own conscience condemns us. Some object here that their consciences do not condemn them. To some extent this may be true; the conscience may be stupefied and perverted through result of previous errors and misconduct.

It is lamentable to be deceived about anything—most of all about this.

2. To deny that we are sinners is to make God a liar.

(a) Because he has expressly and repeatedly declared it. In Romans, Chapter 3, the apostle Paul has gathered dark fragments from many a monument of wickedness, and combined them here into one mournful mosaic, that he might give at least some faint representation of human guilt.

(b) All the arrangements of the plan of salvation presuppose the sin of men, of all men, of every man.

Will you call God a liar? If not, then you are a sinner. Unless we are forgiven, we perish. Let us confess our sins—inwardly, as to God. Ps. 32:5, Prov. 28:13.

II. The provision God has made for our forgiveness.

1. This is consistent with God's justice. This is through the mediation of Christ. Christ is our advocate, our propitiation.

(a) Is the vicarious death of Christ itself consistent with God's justice? Perfectly, when we remember that it was voluntary—"No man taketh it from me; I lay down my life of myself." All the noblest acts of heroism with which Christianity adorned have been of this character—self-sacrifice for others' good. Is his death capable of being accounted for on any other principle? Why could not this cup pass from him?

(b) Does Christ's propitiatory death remove the obstacles to forgiveness? So God's Word declares in John 2:1, 2 and Romans 3:24–26. This atoning death manifests at once God's displeasure with transgression, and his mercy to the transgressor—condemns sin, but saves the sinner. Thus if we confess our sins, we may be forgiven for Jesus' sake.

See then, fellow sinner, that our sins *may* be forgiven, without violating God's justice, without injury to his moral government.

2. But God is pledged that they shall be forgiven.

It is of his mercy, his favor—gratitude so far as we are concerned—but he has pledged himself—his faithfulness to his promises is involved, his equity in fulfilling his engagements.

These promises of God's Word, though they may be familiar, are hope of forgiveness.

Come then to God! Do not deny that you are a sinner, but confess your sins, and seek forgiveness. God's fidelity to his pledged Word is the assurance that he will forgive. Yea, will cleanse from all unrighteousness—will treat us at once as if we were not unrighteous, and will gradually correct and remove our personal unrighteousness, until at last we shall be perfectly holy in heaven.

Come then for "he that covereth his sins shall not prosper; but whosoever confesseth and forsaketh them shall find mercy." Confess, determine to forsake your sin, and you shall find mercy—for "he is faithful and just" to forgive us our sins, and to cleanse us from all unrighteousness.

21

THE SIN OF UNBELIEF

. . . He that believeth not is condemned already, because he hath not believed in the name of the only begotten Son of God. JOHN 3:18

MEN are too apt to think of sin as residing only in outward actions, and not as well in desires and dispositions—or only of positive transgression, and not of negative sin also. The idea of sin in general is vague and unimpressive. Any particular sin will hardly be applicable to all, and some who are not wholly innocent will excuse themselves by thinking of others much more guilty. But the text presents a sin of which all who hear it are guilty, all without exception, all alike— the sin of unbelief.

I. Unbelief a great sin, because the source or the occasion of all other sins.

1. It is seen in the fall. "Ye shall not surely die"—and the woman began to doubt whether God would fulfill his threatenings—the tree was pleasant looking, the fruit inviting—the prospect of being as God awakened sinful pride—she ate. In unbelief it commenced. This led to disobedience.

2. The Israelites "could not enter in because of unbelief"—they had no sufficient confidence in the divine protection. So when unbelieving messengers made fearful report, the people refused to enter, and were condemned to wander, that generation to perish in the wilderness.

They did not believe the clear promise of God's blessing, so amply attested, but did believe the exaggerated report of difficulties. Men are ready to believe what falls in with their feelings or their carnal fears, while they are slow to believe what God hath spoken. Unbelief of the truth always connected with the belief of a lie—that earth is better than heaven, sin lovelier than holiness, time more important than eternity. These and a thousand such lies men are believing, and acting accordingly, while the pure light of divine truth shines all unheeded upon them.

3. Unbelief the occasion of other sins—perverted passions and depraved desires may be the inciting cause, yet but for unbelief these would not suffice. With a true faith we should appreciate the evil of all sins, and be impressed with the beauty of holiness—and faith working by love would purify, etc. Unbelief is to the life as a bitter fountain to the stream. An evil heart of unbelief is like a great marsh sending up noxious vapors. Men often see and deplore the evil effects, and try to correct, but in vain.

II. Unbelief a grievous sin in itself.

We are in God's world—we are bound to receive his teachings as truth, to rest upon his promises, and obey his precepts.

But it is unbelief with respect to the Son of God, which is denounced in the text and elsewhere as a flagrant sin. In the text, dignity of Christ's character seems presented as magnifying guilt of unbelief —"the only begotten Son of God." Consider Jesus as the mediator, the offered object of faith, in condescension to our infirmity—consider too his love, sympathy, invitations—and then estimate the sin of rejecting Christ.

This removes all possibility of question as to one's being a sinner— "but now they have no cloak for their sin." Men often seek to cover up their sin beneath the cloak of various pretences and shadowy, vain excuses. But no question about this sin, whether they realize its guilt or not. This of itself is sufficient to condemn! Would you know your standing before God? There is no need to argue concerning your various excellencies and faults, comparing with others, extenuating and excusing—the text settles the question. Suppose the catalogue of your sins were read to decide your character before God. Whenever this sin is reached, "he hath not believed," etc., then and there the examination will cease, the question is decided. Already, without examining further, the man is condemned.

This is true, dear friends who are unconverted, of you all. As Peter on the day of Pentecost spoke to the people, so would I to you. He did not stop to accuse them of particular sins, nor to consider how much merit there might be in particular excellencies, he did not speak of all that terrible wickedness which then so much abounded, nor of Pharisaic pride nor of Sadducean skepticism—he dwelt upon their rejection of Jesus, the Son of God, both Lord and Christ. It was the consciousness of this crowning sin that pricked them to the heart, and made them cry, etc. And so now. I do not stop to speak of vices, nor even of general alienation of heart—I solemnly say, what God's Word declares, you are condemned as unbelievers in Christ. We may recognize your personal worth in many respects, but you have been rejecting Christ. Often his salvation has been offered, and you have refused to accept it. Do not say you are not an avowed infidel—without that, one may be guilty of unbelief—without that, the Scriptures declare you are guilty.

But some one may say, how can unbelief be a sin (though this Scripture declares it), when I cannot help it? I am unable to believe. The Saviour said, "No man can come unto me," etc. Ah, my friend, do not deceive yourself by that specious excuse.

The Scripture also said, "Ye will not come," etc.—are not willing. If a man is unable to believe, it is only because he is unwilling. Inability is not like that to fly to the stars, nor to know the future—not to lack capacity, but unwillingness. And does this diminish guilt? The more opposed a man is to doing his duty, the more he is blameworthy. If a servant neglects a plain duty, does his lack of inclination exculpate him? The more averse is one's heart to Christ, the more unwilling he is to beileve, so much the greater must be the guiltiness of unbelief. No, no, you are verily guilty.

But why this argument and appeal? Why, might someone say, does a man who wishes others to be happy, labor to convince them that they are very sinful, condemned to destruction? Why should it be said of the Comforter, that he would convince the world of sin? Is there any comfort in such a conviction? Is it not more pleasant, is it not wiser, to forget sin and judgment, than to be reminded of it? No, for this conviction may lead to Him who forgives sin. The man who feels it true of himself that he is condemned already, may know that other gracious truth that "there is no condemnation," etc. "He that believeth on Jesus is not condemned." That very sin of unbelief, which seals your condemnation, may suggest the way of pardon. Cease to reject Jesus, receive him as your Saviour. Acknowledging guilt, pray for mercy, through him. Jesus is able to save you! Will you ask him to save you, and continue to ask? Oh, that you would!

22

THE TWO ROADS OF LIFE

Enter ye in at the strait gate: for wide is the gate, and broad is the way, that leadeth to destruction, and many there be which go in thereat: because strait is the gate, and narrow is the way, which leadeth unto life, and few there be that find it. MATTHEW 7:13, 14

THIS is an appalling generalization when we find that all the countless diversities of human character, conduct, destiny, can be reduced to two classes. Men are diverse—as leaves of the cut-paper mulberry, no two precisely alike. Moreover, they pride themselves so on certain of their diversities and distinctions. Yet they all belong to one or other of two classes. There are but two ways, and two ends they reach. Our Saviour has contrasted these ways in several most important and interesting particulars.

I. Two ways: wide—strait, broad—narrow.

1. The one gate is wide—the entrance upon a wicked life is easy, almost spontaneous—all men begin it in early life. Terrible indeed is the depravity of man, when prone "as the sparks to fly upward," so man easily follows a particular evil course.

But the other is difficult of entrance. For man as he is, and unaided, it is not easy to be converted—he may change some points of outward conduct, may modify disposition, etc—but to effect a radical change is for him impossible. Man forgets the need of divine influence. It is hard to give up self-reliance, as well as to renounce the world.

2. The one way is broad, spacious. As was said before, it is but to yield to natural inclinations. It requires little effort, and no constraint. This broad way "admits of many subdivisions"—may be profligate, or outwardly moral—coarse or refined—a reviler of religion, or a hypocritical pretender to religion. Among a thousand courses, one may take his choice, and yet be still in the broad way.

But the other way is narrow. The Christian life on earth is surpassingly difficult—viewed with carnal eye seems surprisingly disagreeable.

(a) Sometimes the Christian faces opposition, both open or secret —the days of persecution not wholly past.

(b) Many temptations come from wicked acquaintance—for there are human tempters, sometimes through little more than thoughtless folly.

(c) However, worse than either, is one's own inclinations. It costs painful and sustained effort to deny ourselves all sinful gratification, and steadfastly resist the world's allurements. One thoroughly in earnest, striving to climb the heights of holiness, must know that it is difficult.

(d) In addition, one of the chief sources of difficulty and distress in the Christian course, is our own disposition to despondency—we grow fainthearted. Sometimes such despondency is the natural reaction from excessive confidence, or rather from self-confidence. The remedy is prayer—the afflicted pray and sing cheerful psalms.

I would mention many other courses of difficulty—they are legion —and our only help is in the name of the Lord. "Be strong in the Lord, and in the power of his might."

II. Those who travel their ways.

1. One group—and a majority, takes the broad way. Many are taking the wrong road. It is not self-righteous pride to say this, for Jesus said it.

2. A second group—and a small group, only a few, takes the right way. It seems impossible that only a few will see. But this is the clear teaching of the text.

III. The end of the two ways.

1. The one, though broad and crowded, leadeth to destruction. Not the destruction of existence, but of happy existence—not of being, but of well-being. Scriptures speak of death in the strongest terms, to describe the ruin and wretchedness of the world of woe. Jesus himself, so gentle and sympathizing, has often spoken strongly of hell: certainly something as bad as "fire."

2. But the narrow way, though found by few, and difficult, leads to life, [the kind of life given by Jesus]. This will make amends for sacrifice and suffering . . . . And is not the end of any earthly course most important? We are immortal beings. Do you believe indeed that you are to live forever? And shall not this outweigh [all else]?

Hear then the Saviour's injunction—"Enter ye in at the strait gate." Be not deterred by its difficulties—it may seem at first almost impossible, certainly disagreeable. We know this is so—count the cost—

III   As to the end of the two ways

The one, though broad & crowded, leadeth
to destruction. Not the destruct. of existence, but of happy existence — not of being,
but of well-being. — Scriptures employ
death &c. as strongest terms, to describe
... ruin & wretchedness of world of woe.
Jesus himself, so ... gentle & sympathizing,
has often spoken strongly of hell. Certainly
something as bad as fire &c.

But the narrow way, though found by
few, & ... difficult, leads to life.
This as before. This will make amends for
sacrifice & suffering. "Though painful at
present," &c. "no way they flight from star to
star" &c.

And is not the end of any earthly
course most important? We are immortal
beings. Do you believe indeed that you
are to live forever? And shall not this
outweigh &c.?

Hear then the Saviour's injunction,
— "Enter ye in at the strait gate." Be not
deterred by its difficulties — it may seem at
first almost impossible, certainly disagreeable. We do know this is so — count the
cost — but is it not better to ... this than
hell? — To forsake fleeting & imperfect pleasure & ease, rather than turn &c. way to
heaven? — And he who does this
will ... soon find pleasure in so doing —
as one who by an effort leaves the beaten,
crowded way along a mountain's base, &
climbs a narrow path well-nigh alone — pleasure not only in the prospect, but fresh air
making vigorous & buoyant, in the very effort
of climbing the rugged path. So, with
changed desires & tastes, the narrow way
may become a delight.
Enter in quickly — no need, no reason, for
delay. You may become a X'n speedily — Why not
today resolved, in the fear of God, to "deny yourself"
&c.?

Specimen page from Dr. Broadus' pulpit notes

but is it not better to bear this than hell? To forsake fleeting and imperfect pleasure and ease, rather than turn from the way to heaven? And he who does this will soon find pleasure in so doing—as one who by an effort leaves the beaten, crowded way along a mountain's base, and climbs a narrow path well-nigh alone. Pleasure is not only in the prospect, but fresh air and the very effort of climbing the rugged path make one vigorous and bouyant. So, with changed desires and tastes, the narrow way may become a delight.

Enter in quickly—no need, no reason, for delay. You may become a Christian speedily—why not today resolve, in the fear of God, to "deny yourself" and to receive Christ.

23

JESUS: SAVIOUR

And thou shalt call his name Jesus for he shall save his people
from their sins. MATTHEW 1:21

IT is familiar fact that Hebrew names were commonly significant—a
natural and pleasing custom. This being no longer a usage with us,
we often give names of great and good men who have lived in other
days. Sometimes heroes of fiction. This too is beautiful. Names often
make an impression upon those who bear them. So with many who
have borne the names of warriors, orators; sometimes of preachers,
and other good men. But names have often been falsified; and more
often, there are those who dishonor some renowned and venerable
name which has been given to them. These things are not wholly unimportant. And especially might we observe that one name, not individual, but of a party, is often borne in vain—the name Christian.
Truly it is many times "a word and nothing more."

But the name here directed to be given was not in vain The word
Jesus means Saviour. And truly did he become a Saviour. He is Jesus
Christ, the Saviour anointed—he ever lives to save. In the reasons
assigned for giving him this name, there are taught great and glorious
truths. Let us attend to them.

I. He shall save. Emphatic in the original.

1. He, and not we ourselves, save us. We could not have accomplished the work. And it is not a joint affair, by the union of his merit
and ours. He alone saves.

2. He is the Saviour, and not our faith in him. Danger of exalting
faith into an agency, and giving it credit for our salvation, while it
is but a relation to him. Faith ought not to be regarded as a meritorious work, "paying part of our debt." Such an expression is most
unfortunate. He is the author of eternal salvation. Let us not think
there is merit in ordinances, nor in exercises, but Jesus is the Saviour.
Let us look to him, receive him, submit to him, make him our all and
in all.

3. He is to be seen, not as exalted, but as humbled—not as living a life of splendor, but as dying a death of shame. The expectations of his earthly friends were to be disappointed; his cherished, even strengthening hopes to be blasted, but when the sword of acutest suffering was piercing his soul, *then* would he be accomplishing his great work, *thus* becoming the author of salvation. Jesus Christ, and him crucified—the climax of his life, the center of his work.

Of his death alone did he appoint a memorial—not of his miracles, not of his brief hour of seeming earthly triumph, but his disciples in all ages must meet and eat bread and drink wine to "show forth the Lord's death." Yes, it is our dying Lord that is the Saviour—yet not *dead,* for he rose again, he burst the bars of death, he is alive forevermore.

He then shall save. In his own discourses we observe what with reverence may be called a sublime and holy egotism. Fitly does he speak of himself, for he is the Lord and with beginning and end, author and finisher. In him be our trust, to him the glory—yea, his beloved name shall be in the chorus of the everlasting song.

II. He shall save his people. No longer in a national sense, as the Jews would have supposed. "He gave himself for us, that he might redeem us from all iniquity, and purify etc. a peculiar people," etc. All that receive him, that believe on his name become his people—"power to become the sons of God." What an honor, what a happiness, to be of the people of Jesus! The Queen of Sheba thought that Solomon's servants were blessed. How much more are they happy who belong to the people of God, heirs apparent to thrones and crowns in heaven, joint heirs with Jesus Christ, and already blessed with angels as ministering spirits. So angels as they come on their missions of love, with what interest may we suppose them to gaze on those here and there whom they know to be heirs of salvation. They are sadly few, yet found in every rank and condition—in kings' palaces, and wandering in the wilderness—rich like Abraham, or poor like him whom the angels bore to Abraham's bosom—learned and ignorant, master and servant—yea, now in every quarter of the globe —with their diverse languages and customs, etc., yet they love Jesus and serve him, they are his people, greatly blessed now, and to be greatly exalted hereafter.

Who of you would not be of his people? Then come to Jesus; turn, quickly now, unto the Lord, receive Christ as your Saviour.

III. From their sins.

1. From the penalty of their sins. It is well to reflect upon and seek to realize the awful truth that we deserve to die, to suffer

eternal damnation. Suppose we should reflect upon it, each for himself. "I have sinned against God—I know I have." Excuse and extenuate as I may, I know I am a sinner. I deserve to suffer the penalty—to be consigned forever to the damnation of hell. I do not fully know what that will be; but remorse itself will be terrible—remorse, etc. And then positive punishment—something as bad as an undying worm, and quenchless fire. And I cannot cease to sin—and if I could, what shall make amends for my past sin? Ah yes, my friends, we all deserve to perish—but Jesus! he died to save us from perdition. Let us flee to him.

2. From the dominion of sin.

Ye shall die in your sins, a most terrible doom. It were a very inadequate salvation merely to be delivered from positive punishment, and be left sinful. If we have right ideas of sin, we must greatly desire to be saved from our sins. And this Jesus came to accomplish. (a) If we love him, we have new motives to resist our sinful tendencies. (b) Jesus has procured for them that believe on him the special indwelling of the Holy Spirit the Sanctifier. For his gracious influences we may pray, and hope to become more and more holy—to gain more and more the mastery over our sinful dispositions, till the hour of death shall be the hour of perfect deliverance, and we enter upon an eternal existence of sinlessness, of purity. That, that will be heaven.

24

THE GREAT INVITATION

> And the Spirit and the bride say, Come. And let him that heareth say, Come, and let him that is athirst come. And whosoever will, let him take the water of life freely. REVELATION 22:17

THE book of Revelation sets forth the progress of Christianity—its struggles, its reverses, its traits, its final triumph. Now at the close of the book, and of all God's teaching to men, is given this final invitation. With full knowledge of what awaits them, men are invited to come. Jesus, in his own person, as in the beginning of the book, here speaks. Often, when on earth, Jesus had said, "Come." So now, the revelation from on high closes with the same invitation.

It might seem that men would need only an intimation that they may come and would joyfully accept. But they are slow to come, and in infinite condescension and compassion, the invitations are multiplied.

I. Consider those who offer the invitations.

1. The Spirit of God invites men to come.

(a) The Scriptures, which he has inspired, abound in invitations.

(b) The Spirit by his own special influence leads men. Led by his spirit he does draw men so that they shall come. He draws them in a thousand ways—everything calculated to impress the heart, to arouse the conscience, to convince the judgment—is a part of that divine drawing. For observe, "I drew them with cords of a man with bonds of love." He draws us with influences suited to our nature—not as inanimate matter—not as irrational animals—but as men, with cords of a man. Oh, how often do men resist his drawings, withstand all his influences, and perish, complaining all the while, that men did not come, because not drawn.

2. The Bride. The church, including all true Christians of every age, offers an invitation.

146

(a) All efforts of Christians to do good form a continual invitation.

(b) The example of all earnest consistent Christians offers a silent invitation. The fact is that many become Christian, and truly live as such, whom we might have supposed beyond the reach of the gospel whether too bad or too good.

(c) Very many devote themselves to the work of urging this invitation.

3. And let him that heareth say, come. How forcibly does this exhibit the freeness of the invitation. The Saviour desires it to be spread among all men.

II. Who are invited?

1. Let him that is athirst come. Is a man convinced, whether for brief or protracted experiment, that polluted fountains of sinful good cannot satisfy the thirstings of the immortal soul? Not sensuality, not fame, not even knowledge?

Does he believe that there is a good, for this life and that which is to come, that can satisfy and endure?

Does he thirst for this? We ought to desire it—more than anything else, all things else. Many do desire it—at times, for a season, feebly, with distracted desires. Young man who came to Christ, "What shall I do that I may inherit eternal life?" He was not thoroughly in earnest, or he would have partaken. Whosoever then thirsts, let him take.

But this might be misunderstood, as limiting the freeness of the offer. And it is added.

2. Whosoever will. As if carefully guarding against all misunderstanding, anyone who will is invited to come.

(a) Nothing else which man needs or desires, is promised as sure to be obtained. With other things there is still uncertainty. But here, here only, whosoever will may take, whosoever will shall surely receive.

(b) "If I only had become a Christian." "Whosoever will." "I do want to be a Christian"—"whosoever will." "I am so unworthy" —"whosoever will." "I have done my best"—this may be an excuse, "whosoever will." "I am not fit to come"—"come freely."

Many things call you away—but oh, heed the invitation of the text. And make up your mind that you will *come* to Christ.